NEW DIRECTIONS FOR YOUTH DEVELOPMENT

Theory
Practice
Research

winter | 2011

Support and Instruction for Youth Purpose

Jenni Menon Mariano | *issue editor*

Gil G. Noam
Editor-in-Chief

JOSSEY-BASS™
An Imprint of
WILEY

SUPPORT AND INSTRUCTION FOR YOUTH PURPOSE
Jenni Menon Mariano (ed.)
New Directions for Youth Development, No. 132, Winter 2011
Gil G. Noam, Editor-in-Chief
This is a peer-reviewed journal.

Copyright © 2012 Wiley Periodicals, Inc., A Wiley Company. All rights reserved. No part of this publication may be reproduced in any form or by any means, except as permitted under sections 107 and 108 of the 1976 United States Copyright Act, without either the prior written permission of the publisher or authorization through the Copyright Clearance Center, 222 Rosewood Drive, Danvers, MA 01923; (978) 750-8400; fax (978) 646-8600. The copyright notice appearing at the bottom of the first page of an article in this journal indicates the copyright holder's consent that copies may be made for personal or internal use, or for personal or internal use of specific clients, on the condition that the copier pay for copying beyond that permitted by law. This consent does not extend to other kinds of copying, such as copying for general distribution, for advertising or promotional purposes, for creating collective works, or for resale. Such permission requests and other permission inquiries should be addressed to the Permissions Department, c/o John Wiley & Sons, Inc., 111 River Street, Hoboken, NJ 07030; (201) 748-6011, fax (201) 748-6008, www.wiley.com/go/permissions.

Microfilm copies of issues and articles are available in 16mm and 35mm, as well as microfiche in 105mm, through University Microfilms Inc., 300 North Zeeb Road, Ann Arbor, MI 48106-1346.

New Directions for Youth Development is indexed in Academic Search (EBSCO), Academic Search Premier (EBSCO), Contents Pages in Education (T&F), Current Abstracts (EBSCO), Educational Research Abstracts Online (T&F), EMBASE/Excerpta Medica (Elsevier), ERIC Database (Education Resources Information Center), Index Medicus/MEDLINE/PubMed (NLM), MEDLINE/PubMed (NLM), SocINDEX (EBSCO), Sociology of Education Abstracts (T&F), and Studies on Women & Gender Abstracts (T&F).

NEW DIRECTIONS FOR YOUTH DEVELOPMENT (ISSN 1533-8916, electronic ISSN 1537-5781) is part of the Jossey-Bass Psychology Series and is published quarterly by Wiley Subscription Services, Inc., A Wiley Company, at Jossey-Bass, One Montgomery Street, Suite 1200, San Francisco, CA 94104-4594. POSTMASTER: Send address changes to New Directions for Youth Development, Jossey-Bass, One Montgomery Street, Suite 1200, San Francisco, CA 94104-4594.

SUBSCRIPTIONS for individuals cost $89.00 for U.S./Canada/Mexico; $113.00 international. For institutions, agencies, and libraries, $281.00 U.S.; $321.00 Canada/Mexico; $355.00 international. Prices subject to change. Refer to the order form that appears at the back of most volumes of this journal.

EDITORIAL CORRESPONDENCE should be sent to the Editor-in-Chief, Dr. Gil G. Noam, McLean Hospital, Harvard Medical School, 115 Mill Street, Belmont, MA 02478.

Cover photograph by David H. Lewis/©iStockphoto

Gil G. Noam, Editor-in-Chief
Harvard University and McLean Hospital

Editorial Board

K. Anthony Appiah
Princeton University
Princeton, N.J.

Peter Benson
Search Institute
Minneapolis, Minn.

Dale A. Blyth
University of Minnesota
Minneapolis, Minn.

Dante Cicchetti
University of Minnesota
Minneapolis, Minn.

William Damon
Stanford University
Palo Alto, Calif.

Goéry Delacôte
At-Bristol Science Museum
Bristol, England

Felton Earls
Harvard Medical School
Boston, Mass.

Jacquelynne S. Eccles
University of Michigan
Ann Arbor, Mich.

Wolfgang Edelstein
Max Planck Institute for Human Development
Berlin, Germany

Kurt Fischer
Harvard Graduate School of Education
Cambridge, Mass.

Carol Gilligan
New York University Law School
New York, N.Y.

Robert Granger
W. T. Grant Foundation
New York, N.Y.

Ira Harkavy
University of Philadelphia
Philadelphia, Penn.

Reed Larson
University of Illinois at Urbana-Champaign
Urbana-Champaign, Ill.

Richard Lerner
Tufts University
Medford, Mass.

Milbrey W. McLaughlin
Stanford University
Stanford, Calif.

Pedro Noguera
New York University
New York, N.Y.

Fritz Oser
University of Fribourg
Fribourg, Switzerland

Karen Pittman
The Forum for Youth Investment
Washington, D.C.

Jane Quinn
The Children's Aid Society
New York, N.Y.

Jean Rhodes
University of Massachusetts, Boston
Boston, Mass.

Rainer Silbereisen
University of Jena
Jena, Germany

Elizabeth Stage
University of California at Berkeley
Berkeley, Calif.

Hans Steiner
Stanford Medical School
Stanford, Calif.

Carola Suárez-Orozco
New York University
New York, N.Y.

Marcelo Suárez-Orozco
New York University
New York, N.Y.

Erin Cooney, Editorial Manager
Program in Education, Afterschool and Resiliency (PEAR)

Discover this journal online at
wileyonlinelibrary.com

Contents

Issue Editor's Notes

AS THE STUDY OF youth purpose has progressed over the past decade or so, researchers and practitioners have become increasingly concerned with understanding the characteristics of environments and curricula that support its development. And they have good reason for having such an interest. The emergence of noble purpose in one's youth is associated with several positive characteristics, including psychological adjustment and well-being, personal development, hope, life satisfaction, empathy, gratitude, generosity, and meaning in life and in one's work.

If this list does not convince us that purpose should be systematically supported, it is useful to know that the benefits of purpose are further embodied in what it does for both the person and society at large. Noble purposes are stable goals that matter to the young person who has them; moreover, they connect that young person to matters that are greater than himself or herself. According to research on purpose in today's American youth, these greater matters include social causes, country, family, faith, the arts, and work, to name a just a few. Whatever the content of one's noble purposes, the point is that having that purpose in life helps the young person forge a unity between matters of self and other. Purpose builds a link between one's personal interests and activities and that innate human desire to make a significant difference to the social context in which one lives. Purpose thus provides an authentic pathway for youth to concomitantly serve interests of self and community. Particularly for American youth, this authenticity is key because it is a response to Western ways of thinking that traditionally separate interests for self and other.

NEW DIRECTIONS FOR YOUTH DEVELOPMENT, NO. 132, WINTER 2011 © WILEY PERIODICALS, INC.
Published online in Wiley Online Library (wileyonlinelibrary.com) • DOI: 10.1002/yd.423

Several other compelling facts of a more sociological nature portend a focus on supporting youth purpose in research, policy, and practice. First, changes in the life span of the U.S. population over the past twenty years have significantly extended the period from childhood to adulthood. It has created a longer period of moratorium during which young people are pressed to form life agendas. This extended period places greater emphasis on finding meaningful purposes that youth can act on in the moment and are not just related to what they will accomplish when they become adults. We can add to this the recent global economic downturn that has significantly affected young people's opportunities in career development and higher education, and it is not uncommon to find that many youth find forming a positive vision of their future a challenge. In fact, recent studies suggest that only a small percentage of youngsters at any age are able to form positive purposes.

Unfortunately, some writers and voices in the media explain away the apparent purposelessness of today's youth by problematizing the younger generation. Many attribute negative qualities to today's youth that they claim predispose them to purposelessness. But to accept this explanation not only marginalizes young people, but it risks missing out on making important educational, research, and policy gains for positive youth and community development— and ones that would promote well-being for people of all ages. In contrast, the articles in this volume of *New Directions for Youth Development* are countercultural. Instead of blaming today's youth for the sociological trends, they focus on addressing whole community practices within the contexts in which American youth live.

Several of the articles in this volume stem from youth purpose research conducted at the Stanford Center on Adolescence by William Damon and supported by the John Templeton Foundation and the Thrive Foundation for Youth. These studies examine the forms, frequency, and thriving correlates of purpose by surveying and interviewing cohorts of adolescents and emerging adults across the United States over several years. Thus, a focus on the features and outcomes of purpose is well established. A critical next step is to gain insight into the social supports of purpose and how these supports can be translated into educational practice.

The articles that follow discuss practical implications for supporting purpose. The key question addressed is what kinds of learning tools and experiences are most likely to foster positive purpose. This groundbreaking research is among the first to explicitly address the supports of youth purpose and to construct youth purpose interventions. Thus this volume presents the current state of the field on instructing for youth purpose and serves as a resource for researchers, policymakers, teachers, and other practitioners who are interested in promoting positive youth development and thriving.

Some of the articles are analyses of data collected through multiple waves of the Stanford youth purpose studies, and others are independent research developed in part through Stanford youth purpose award grants to the article authors. Each article uses the notion of purpose as an intentionally constructed, stable, and higher-order goal that is meaningful to self yet expressed in actions that have a positive impact on others. This idea of purpose is explicitly invoked by each of the authors in this volume and thus provides a backdrop for the study of purpose supports.

Sonia Issac Koshy and Jenni Menon Mariano's review of research on purpose support and programs in the opening article reveals where rather large gaps in the youth purpose education literature lie. One might ask whether it is too early to review the literature on teaching for purpose given the dearth of current research on the topic that these authors find. However, they show how vital it is for educators to know about tools previously used to teach for purpose. They also highlight themes imperative for follow-up by researchers and educators. Indeed, several purpose programs have been used in the past, and although they are no longer in use, they can be replicated by practitioners today. Furthermore, the authors show that several strategies currently being used to teach for positive youth development in general can help lay a foundation for the formation of purpose.

Kendall Cotton Bronk next discusses how purpose supports, and is supported by, one specific feature of healthy adolescent development: the formation of identity. Cotton Bronk's article, which focuses on psychological supports of purpose, also sets the stage for the remaining articles by illustrating pictures of young people who serve as purpose exemplars over a five-year period. Thus, an important and preliminary question is addressed for readers unfamiliar with the youth purpose construct: What does purpose look like in diverse groups of young people? Cotton Bronk presents portraits of purpose through vivid and stable examples, drawing from a group of young people nominated as purpose exemplars, and thus exhibiting positive youth purpose in its most glowing forms.

In the third article, Devora Shamah derives valuable insights from a study on supports of purpose among a sample of rural youth. This research shows that traditional out-of-school-time activities, community-based activities, and work experiences may all be important for developing a strong sense of purpose among this group. Shamah also suggests that lessons from these communities may be applied in urban and suburban communities.

The next three articles report outcomes of purpose interventions designed for formal educational settings differing by age level served. Practitioners can take concrete lessons from each of these articles and adapt them for use in their own educational settings. In article four, Bryan J. Dik, Michael F. Steger, Amanda Gibson, and William Peisner discuss an evaluation of their own self-designed purpose intervention for middle school students. They invoke the idea of work as greater purpose or calling in their purpose-centered career education intervention. Students engage in a three-module-lesson activity aimed at increasing four factors considered critical to the cultivation of purpose in the early stages of career development: identity, self-efficacy, metacognition, culture, and service to the greater good. Next, in the fifth article, Jane Elizabeth Pizzolato, Elizabeth Levine Brown, and Mary Allison Kanny examine the effectiveness of an intervention designed to promote purpose and internal control over academic success in high school students living in a low-socioeconomic-status community. Next, Matthew J. Bundick examines the benefits to college students' goal directedness and life satisfaction that accrue from a one-on-one purpose discussion.

In each case, the authors of these three articles offer fresh approaches to their respective fields by centering their work on the purpose construct in ways that youth purpose researchers have not previously addressed. Dik and his colleagues incorporate instruction in service to the greater good, which is seldom incorporated in career development studies. Pizzolato and her colleagues apply the study of youth purpose to the achievement gap problem, showing that purpose is an important factor often missed in the literature around this issue. Bundick's study fills a gap in intervention research by assessing the effects of a purpose intervention on later purpose and lasting purpose.

Altogether, the articles in this volume underscore several insights about supporting purpose that researchers and youth development practitioners will want to be aware of. First is the socially embedded nature of purpose support—embedded in the sense that multiple environments give rise to this support in adolescents' lives, including in-school-time and out-of-school-time contexts. Shamah's research highlights this theme, as does the work that Isaac Koshy and Menon Mariano review.

A second theme is that purpose support may be best facilitated across time. Educators cannot achieve sustained quality contact with all the students they will teach, however. Fortunately, the research shows that small and short-term interventions can be effective. This is important given the current high-stakes testing environment and the increasing class sizes that many schools have experienced. It is no wonder that, given these conditions, teachers feel that teaching for purpose constitutes an "extra," a luxury, or goes beyond their training. Bundick highlights the user friendliness of a reflection and discussion approach to promoting purpose that does not require any advanced expertise and that students can be encouraged to use themselves. Thus, educators should take heart that they can successfully support students' purposes through even short classroom intervals, as well as through long-term contact.

Finally, an important theme delineated in this volume is that youth from all walks of life experience purpose. Young purpose exemplars are diverse in age, ethnicity, academic achievement, and gender, and they take on a variety of causes, ranging from saving the environment to creating beautiful music. Instruction for purpose, whether formal or informal, can succeed for youth living in low-income communities, urban and rural environments, and those attending schools at different levels. As the article authors in this volume show, there are now a number of innovative approaches to instructing for youth purpose that are being studied, and these provide a platform on which researchers and practitioners can build. In the concluding article, Menon Mariano discusses specific ways that researchers, practitioners, and policymakers can build on the platform of these studies.

I thank Gil G. Noam and Erin Cooney for their support of this volume, as well as all the article authors. This work would not have been accomplished without the pioneering work of William Damon and the financial support for the initial youth purpose studies by the John Templeton Foundation, and the Thrive Foundation for Youth.

Jenni Menon Mariano
Issue Editor

JENNI MENON MARIANO *is an assistant professor of educational psychology and human development at the University of South Florida Sarasota-Manatee.*

Executive Summary

Chapter One: Promoting youth purpose: A review of the literature

Sonia Issac Koshy, Jenni Menon Mariano

This article reviews the research literature on teaching and supporting purpose in adolescence and young adulthood. An extensive search revealed that most studies on youth purpose examine psychological correlates and neglect instructional and social supports. School is an effective context for fostering purpose, yet reported approaches for explicitly instructing for purpose are rare after the early 1990s, reflecting a trend away from a language of purpose as a discrete endeavor in education since at least the 1960s. Furthermore, research on the outcomes of early purpose instruction curricula is not present in empirical journal articles. Nevertheless, a concern for fostering youth purpose has not disappeared from education; rather, it is subsumed under approaches that foster more comprehensive positive student outcomes, such as character, civic engagement, and positive youth development. Key curricular approaches to these outcomes are therefore also reviewed and examined for insights into how purpose can be fostered.

Chapter Two: The role of purpose in life in healthy identity formation: A grounded model

Kendall Cotton Bronk

Researchers contend that committing to an inspiring purpose in life is an important component of healthy identity development for

NEW DIRECTIONS FOR YOUTH DEVELOPMENT, NO. 132, WINTER 2011 © WILEY PERIODICALS, INC.
Published online in Wiley Online Library (wileyonlinelibrary.com) • DOI: 10.1002/yd.424

adolescents; however, little research has focused on how identity and purpose develop together. Therefore, the study followed a sample of eight adolescent purpose exemplars for five years in order to develop a grounded model of the way these two constructs interact. Findings suggest that for adolescent purpose exemplars, the processes of identity formation and purpose development reinforce one another; the development of purpose supports the development of identity, and the development of identity reinforces purposeful commitments. Furthermore, in the adolescent purpose exemplars' lives, the purpose and identity constructs largely overlap in such a way that what individuals hope to accomplish in their lives serves as the basis of the adults they hope to become. Implications of these findings are discussed.

Chapter Three: Supporting a strong sense of purpose: Lessons from a rural community

Devora Shamah

Many rural youth leave their small home towns, at least temporarily, to pursue education and work opportunities after high school. A strong sense of purpose will likely help these young people navigate their transition to adulthood away from the comforts of home. A case study of high school students in a remote rural county in the Pacific Northwest using survey and ethnographic data showed that traditional out-of-school activities (for example, sports, theater, band, Future Farmers of America) and community-based activities (for example, community symphony, community classes, community events), along with work experiences, were all important for developing a strong sense of purpose. The case study points to the important role small rural schools can play in supporting youth and connecting them to activities that foster a strong sense of purpose. In addition, this article discusses the importance of paying attention to the development of a sense of purpose alongside traditional measures of academic achievement and social competence.

Chapter Four: Make Your Work Matter: Development and pilot evaluation of a purpose-centered career education intervention

Bryan J. Dik, Michael F. Steger, Amanda Gibson, William Peisner

Developing a sense of purpose is both salient and desirable for adolescents, and purpose in people's lives and careers is associated with both general and work-related well-being. However, little is known about whether purpose can be encouraged through school-based interventions. This article reports the results of a quasi-experimental pilot study and follow-up focus group that evaluated Make Your Work Matter, a three-module, school-based intervention designed to help adolescent youth explore, discover, and enact a sense of purpose in their early career development. Participants were eighth-grade students. Compared to the control group, the intervention group reported increases in several outcomes related to purpose-centered career development, such as a clearer sense of career direction; a greater understanding of their interests, strengths, and weaknesses; and a greater sense of preparedness for the future. However, no significant differences were found on items directly related to purpose, calling, and prosocial attitudes. These results inform the ongoing development of Make Your Work Matter and other school-based career interventions and pave the way for larger-scale trials of such purpose-promoting intervention strategies.

NEW DIRECTIONS FOR YOUTH DEVELOPMENT • DOI: 10.1002/yd

Chapter Five: Purpose plus: Supporting youth purpose, control, and academic achievement

Jane Elizabeth Pizzolato, Elizabeth Levine Brown,
Mary Allison Kanny

Research in the past decade suggests that a persistent achievement gap between students from low-income minority backgrounds and higher-income white backgrounds may be rooted in theories of student motivation and youth purpose. Yet limited research exists regarding the role of purpose on positive youth development as it pertains to academic achievement. Using a sample of 209 high school students, this study examines the effectiveness of an intervention designed to promote purpose development and internal control over academic success in high school students from a low-socioeconomic-status community. Findings reveal that a short-term intervention was effective in significantly increasing internal control over academic success and purpose in life for students participating in the intervention group. In addition, analysis of academic achievement for students who experienced positive gains in internal control and purpose demonstrates significant gains in academic achievement as measured by grade point average. Implications are made for further study of internal control and life purpose as a means of academic intervention in the effort to address the achievement gap.

Chapter Six: The benefits of reflecting on and discussing purpose in life in emerging adulthood

Matthew J. Bundick

The benefits of understanding and pursuing one's purposes in life are well documented. However, few studies have addressed potential interventions for enhancing purpose. This article presents the results of an empirical investigation testing whether reflecting on and discussing one's core values, life goals, and purposes in life has benefits for later purpose, as well as later life satisfaction. The study involved a pretest/posttest experimental design with 102 college students, with posttest measures administered nine months later. Results showed that those who engaged in the guided discussion of their values, life goals, and purpose (compared to those who did not) benefited in terms of their goal directedness and life satisfaction and that the benefits for life satisfaction were partially attributable to changes in goal directedness. The article concludes by highlighting implications for practitioners of all kinds, including parents, with recommendations for implementing the purpose discussion in a variety of youth settings.

Chapter Seven: Conclusion: Recommendations for how practitioners, researchers, and policymakers can promote youth purpose

Jenni Menon Mariano

Initially drawing from, yet then expanding on the research discussed in this volume, this article discusses specific measures that practitioners, researchers, and policymakers can take to support purpose among youth. Strategies for educators include utilizing practical purpose teaching tools, such as purpose interviews, purpose-related discussions, whole classroom and school community games, and purpose survey methodologies. Research strategies include expanding the study of youth purpose to more diverse groups of young people, and developing more succinct tools to assess purpose in research. Finally, the article discusses policy measures to promote purpose, including modification of current academic testing practices, expanding the breadth of course and extracurricular experiences in schools to provide opportunities for purpose development, and integrating purpose promotion skill-building into existing teacher education programs.

The authors examine the research literature on teaching for youth purpose in formal and informal educational contexts.

1

Promoting youth purpose: A review of the literature

Sonia Issac Koshy, Jenni Menon Mariano

ADOLESCENCE HAS LONG been considered a period of heightened purpose formation. According to Damon, Menon, and Bronk, purpose is an intention to accomplish something that is both important to the self and directed at making a difference in the world beyond self, usually in a positive way.[1] Studies of purpose exemplars, for instance, profile young people who express commitment to diverse social goals, ranging from civic causes like improving people's lives through preserving the environment or finding cures for disease, to making a significant contribution to the arts.[2] Purpose is an organizing principle, providing young people with a coherent vision of their future that connects in meaningful ways to their present life. So, for example, purpose can infuse young people's otherwise seemingly mundane everyday activities, like schoolwork, with a heightened sense of motivation, relevance, and direction. The young person who previously found schoolwork boring might now, with a new purpose, view academic achievement as a pathway to fulfilling vocational dreams. In this way, purpose provides focus and motivation, staves off boredom, and

NEW DIRECTIONS FOR YOUTH DEVELOPMENT, NO. 132, WINTER 2011 © WILEY PERIODICALS, INC.
Published online in Wiley Online Library (wileyonlinelibrary.com) • DOI: 10.1002/yd.425

galvanizes young people's commitments in the here and now to both existing and future achievements.

It is not surprising that young people who have found a positive purpose not only show decreases in negative outcomes but are more likely to thrive. Furthermore, having a purpose goes beyond personal benefits. The beyond-the-self quality of purpose can help adolescents think beyond personal gains and help promote moral actions for the sake of others. This focus on others is essential to societal progress and survival.[3] Given the value of youth purpose to both self and society, it is essential for educators to understand what they can do to foster purpose. The central question of this review, therefore, is: How can positive purpose be supported and taught in formal and informal educational contexts?

Method

We began a search of peer-reviewed journal articles in English by using the subject and keyword search term *purpose* on the databases of PsychINFO, the Education Resources Information Center, Social Sciences Full Text, and Web of Science. We retained articles pertaining to adolescents and young adults and discarded those dealing with older populations. Articles were then examined for research on variables associated with teaching and education for purpose and social support and influences of purpose that were studied as either the dependent or outcome variables. Virtually no research assessing curricula to explicitly teach for youth purpose before 1980 was found, although some descriptions of programs from before this period were available. It was found, however, that various other indicators of positive development during adolescence lead to the mutual benefit of self and society in a similar manner to purpose. Therefore, given the conceptual connection of youth purpose by scholars in the literature to themes of character education, civic engagement, and positive youth development, key instructional methods relating to these three areas were examined.

The subject searches yielded 465 articles. The majority of articles did not pertain to purpose as it is conceptualized in this article. So, for example, we discarded articles using the term *purpose* in the everyday sense of the word, such as of a behavior like doing homework or reading. The dominating focus of the remaining research was on psychological correlates of purpose.

Findings

School can support purpose

The research to date reports a positive relationship between purpose and school and teacher support, suggesting that purpose can be fostered by institutions of learning. Adolescents frequently speak about school-related goals when they are asked about their purposes in life. White, Wagener, and Furrow asked male adolescents to describe their purposes in their own words and found that school achievement was the category of purpose that was discussed most frequently among both thriving and at-risk groups.[4] In another study, purpose in life correlated positively and significantly with perceived social support from teachers and school in a sample of adolescent girls.[5] For one, it seems that academic subject matter and skills may be successfully brought to bear on reflecting on and actualizing one's life purpose, even toward prosocial ends. A historical case study by Pletcher of women at Bryn Mawr College during the progressive era, for example, shows how courses in English composition allowed women what was perhaps their first opportunity to craft and express a voice as social reformers, even in the face of social mores that restricted their involvement in those realms.[6]

The research findings also suggest, however, that while many schools may successfully be addressing the aspirational needs of most youngsters, these same schools may be less effectively serving youth who are either lacking or precocious in purpose. In one study, girls with diverse forms of purpose reported support from their school, but this support was significantly greater for girls whose purpose formation was either partial ("dreamer" and "dabbler" forms) or nonexistent than it was for girls with clear purpose ("self-oriented purpose" or "beyond-self purpose" forms).[7] Furthermore, dreamer and dabbler groups tended to place greater value on the support of teachers and schools than did the other purpose groups. Thus, deliberate measures to support purpose for all youngsters are in order.

Few educational programs explicitly teach for purpose

In spite of an apparent need to teach for purpose, our search yielded very few accounts of school programs in the past twenty years that explicitly teach for purpose. We expect that this finding reflects a shift in language away from the discrete terminology of "life purpose" in education, used more frequently in the 1960s, 1970s, and earlier in the twentieth century. But it is even more striking that instructional approaches to teach specifically for purpose are absent from academic research journals. A few documented approaches from earlier time periods, however, are worth noting. For example, articles written by Cernik, by Glasson, by Howell, and by Mueller in the late 1960s and early 1970s describe a program developed in the 1950s.[8] The program was conducted in conjunction with the 1965 Character Research Project (CRP) Youth Congress and later integrated into at least one counseling program in a junior high school, as well as piloted at youth development agencies and university campuses in the Midwest.

In each case, a distinguishing program feature was participation in multiple activities over a significant period of time, sometimes over the course of years. For instance, prior to the youth congress, participants gathered data about what they individually considered to be their "destiny" or life purpose. Data included an inventory of delegates' interests and activities, choice of their purposes as they pertained to subject or career areas, reports of pre-engagement with the CRP curriculum coauthored with their parents, and interviews with five "Great People" chosen by the delegates because these people were distinguished in an adolescent's life purpose area.[9] During the congress itself, delegates participated in six days of activities related to developing life purpose. Finally, in the year following the congress, participants worked on accomplishing the life purpose goals they had set and providing monthly reports.

In the junior school application of the CRP curriculum, students were called on to reflect on their life purposes and goals in conjunction with activities organized by the school's guidance counselor. Beginning in seventh grade, each student was interviewed by the guidance counselor, who urged them to think deeply about their futures. In eighth grade, students completed an autobiography intended to help them think about who they are and who they will become. They then met with the guidance counselor for ten guided sessions designed to help them develop their purposes and translate them into immediate action. Finally, in ninth grade, students participated in more in-depth career exploration activities.[10] From a more contemporary perspective, the approach described here might be considered quite cutting edge. In 2008, Kosine, Steger, and Duncan argued for promoting purpose-centered career development in high schools, stating that purpose is not an area that is typically cultivated during career exploration activities.[11]

A more recent program is Cohen's purpose-centered system of education, based on a prototype developed in the 1970s, that has since been integrated into a college system, and multiple elementary and middle schools (http://www.mcny.edu/human_serv/bpsabout.php).[12] In the system, schools teach their students to use knowledge of subject matter to identify socially significant purposes. Each semester focuses on a learning stage associated with a socially useful outcome, such as building a better environment or improving service in an institution outside school. Students then together engage in a major project that addresses the social purpose, and their course material is brought to bear on this project. Courses are structured around five themes, or dimensions, that draw on diverse subject matter and align with the notion of purpose discussed in this article. In the first class, titled "Purpose," students learn skills of problem solving, persistence, and flexibility. The remaining classes deal with other aspects of prosocial purpose, including forming constructive relationships between self and other, fostering abilities to operate as members of a global society, and developing practical skills to operate as adult citizens. Each class is directed toward the specific purpose, and in this way the program differs from experiential learning for its own sake. Thus, the basic principle is to merge student action in common, prosocial purposes.[13]

Two features are central to the approaches described here. First is the focus on long-term engagement with purpose-related curricula as opposed to one-lesson or one-classroom approaches. In the schools, the emphasis is on integrating purpose education into curricula, or into the student's school experience throughout the course of a year or years through a series of learning experiences. The second feature is attention to two aspects of developing adolescents' purposes: having adolescents reflect on and form plans around what is important to them and their interests, and connecting adolescents' interests with prosocial ends or larger, common purposes to serve society. These latter two features may appear in different sequences, but they are inseparable; they emphasize the underlying principle that an authentic sense of purpose must connect with a young person's diverse interests and cannot simply be imposed from the outside. The research on social supports of purpose reviewed also emphasizes this point and suggests the bidirectional nature of the relationship between student interest and purposeful social commitment.

School's contribution to purpose is connected to other contexts

Formal and informal educational contexts outside school also support purpose. For this reason, teachers' and schools' contribution to purpose support must be viewed within the broader community contexts in which adolescents are embedded. Worthen, Johnson, Badore, and Bentley found that purpose in life increased, became more realistic, was perceived as more self-directed, and became more prosocial for delinquent boys when they were enrolled in a four-month camp experience.[14] Other research found moderate effects for associations between school and purpose in life, yet these correlations were not significantly different from associations with other supportive contexts, such as parents, close friends, and classmates.[15]

A further examination of purpose-specific supports in interview data showed that highly purposeful adolescents reported more frequent support from multiple people and environments. How people and contexts proffered support is also noteworthy. The highly purposeful adolescents reported more support that was specific to their interests, gave them practical knowledge that they could apply to pursuing their interests, came from people they perceived to be role models and mentors, and emerged through social activities and experiences that were repeated over time and were seen as sociocultural traditions. Furthermore, youth are not passive recipients of purpose support, but actively select support in the service of their chosen purposes.[16] Schools themselves may take lessons from these out-of-school-time findings. Hansell examined academic purpose in a private secondary school and found that educational commitment among students developed when the school environment promotes intensive face-to-face interaction in a primary community, a sense of history and tradition resulting from continuity in educational experiences, and a sense of students' power over their school lives.[17]

How teaching for character, civic engagement, and positive youth development may foster purpose

Few programs explicitly teach for purpose. However, we expect that some approaches may support purpose without a specific focus on the construct. In an attempt to build the knowledge, attitudes, and actions necessary for purpose development, we seek to understand the methods used for character education, civic engagement, and positive youth development (PYD). One cannot merely prescribe positive behaviors as mandated laws in an attempt to instill prosocial characteristics in individuals. Rather, individuals need the skills necessary to pursue purposeful behavior, the internalized motivation to pursue the purposeful behavior, and the follow-through of engaging in purposeful behavior. Accordingly, to socialize youth to pursue purposeful paths, we describe methods used in character education, civic engagement, and PYD that integrate the three essential components for prosocial behavior: changes in cognition (knowledge), affect (motivation), and behavior (action).

Teaching for character

The promotion of character development relies on fostering virtues and morals in youth, especially within schools.[18] Proponents emphasize the importance of integrating character education into established curricula. For example, Berkowitz and Bier suggest building an implicit culture of ethics and care in classrooms through a focus on character, morality, ethics, values, and virtue within readings, lessons, and curricular issues.[19] Furthermore, Berger states that schools need to move toward connecting character education to the lives of students and the world beyond the school community.[20] Therefore, there has been an emphasis on building character in students through service-learning. This bridge between classroom and community is designed to build students' ability to think beyond themselves and increase their sense of social responsibility, and thus, to promote character.[21] Such attempts to develop character have been instantiated in hundreds of programs across the United States.[22]

It is useful to briefly consider the features of character education programs so as to understand how such programs may foster purpose. The Character Education Partnership (CEP) is a nonprofit coalition of organizations and individuals that advocate for quality character education and recognizes various K-12 schools and districts for their achievements in character education each year. Although each program is unique in its curricula and contexts, the objective of the programs is similar: to create a caring community and thereby foster an ethic of care in youth. Indeed, the schools have found that character education has yielded positive results in student behavior, citizenship and leadership, school climate, and academic performance.[23] The diversity of curricula in each school precludes a comprehensive description of all approaches. Nevertheless, the CEP offers a useful summary of the principles on which prototypical effective character education programs should be based. For example, it advocates defining character comprehensively to include thinking, feeling, and behavior and to thus use an intentional yet comprehensive approach to character development that goes beyond merely teaching classroom lessons on the subject. A comprehensive approach includes creating a caring school community that provides students with opportunities for moral action. It requires an academic curriculum that is challenging yet also develops students' character and fosters their self-motivation. Furthermore, it calls for the engagement of entire school communities: all staff, families, and students. Finally, it requires an evaluative component that assesses the performance of the moral atmosphere of the school, including the staff's functioning as character educators and the degree to which students exhibit good character (see http://www.character.org).

Teaching for civic engagement

Although family, faith institutions, media, and social organizations are traditionally held responsible for fostering an individual's civic character and inclination for civic participation, the school helps individuals learn the skills, knowledge, and attitudes to make informed decisions about citizenship.[24] As such, the Center for Civic Education seeks to engage youth to become informed, responsible citizens through the classroom. There are three essential components: civic knowledge, civic skills, and civic disposition.[25] A report outlining the positive influence of civics curricula identified six best practices for promoting engagement in civics: instruction in government with more than rote learning, discussion of current events, opportunities to apply classroom learning through service-learning projects, extracurricular community service, student participation in school governance, and simulation of procedures and the democratic process.[26]

One example of how these practices can be integrated is the use of civics education in classes other than those in social studies. English teachers, for example, can integrate such concepts as personal rights and responsibilities, political rights, economic rights, and civic responsibilities through discussions of books in which such themes arise, and all teachers can promote civic education through student body government.[27] When students observe the workings of democracy within their own classrooms and schools, they are more inclined to respect and carry the rules forward within their own civic lives in the future. In addition, responsibility for the community can be taught through community service projects. Experiential learning can help students become civically minded.[28] Community service can help youth learn about the institution through which they are engaged and its larger social and political context. In addition, supervision of the service and reflection on the experience can help students gain additional knowledge about how to be a good citizen within a democratic society.

Teaching for positive youth development

Positive youth development is an overarching term for an approach that that is closely related to civic and character education. This approach advocates a view of youth as resources to be developed rather than problems to be managed. Thus, it has spurred a new vocabulary to describe the strengths of youth, using such terms as *developmental assets* and *thriving*, as well as *purpose*.[29] These concepts were constructed with the understanding that youth have the potential for successful, healthy development and that each individual has the capability for positive development. Therefore, it is clear that positive purpose falls under this general concept of PYD.

In some cases, it appears that programs that foster PYD also foster purpose. Indeed, adolescents who participate in youth programs have growth in PYD through access to opportunities to learn and build important skills, including purpose.[30] For example, Borden and Serido showed positive outcomes at one youth empowerment center.[31] Drawing on our previous review of programs that explicitly teach for purpose, it is clear that the center

NEW DIRECTIONS FOR YOUTH DEVELOPMENT • DOI: 10.1002/yd

activities combined features of these programs, including a long-term focus and a gradual melding of youths' interests with a beyond-the-self focus. At the center, youth were first brought together through a shared interest that allowed them to establish relationships with peers and adults. As they became more invested, they began to explore connections between the center and the larger community. As their exploration continued, they began to understand the impact of their participation to their personal well-being and the benefit of the surrounding community.

Implications: Bridging our understanding to purpose education

Although *character development*, *civic engagement*, and *PYD* are different terms that have diverse implications for adolescent development, fostering purpose has the potential to lead to these three components of an adolescent's identity. Given that reaching a purposeful life involves knowing what goals to pursue, through the support and instruction of purpose, adolescents can choose activities that develop character, civic engagement, or levels of PYD. It therefore comes as no surprise that through the principles and practices we have described to develop these assets, the instruction and support of purpose can be informed as well. Purpose-driven discussions, experiential and service-learning opportunities, and goal-directed activity engagement with like-minded peers and adults can be used to promote positive purpose in adolescents.

Much like the methods we have noted, we believe that purpose can be promoted in adolescents through the identification of goals, experiencing activities that help to actualize stated goals, and reflecting on the activities and how they relate to the bigger picture of life purpose that youth have identified for themselves. When young people are able to set prosocial goals and target the steps needed to reach the goal, they can work to change their orientation to the world, and thus attain a commitment to pursuing their life purpose. Therefore, it may be that a commitment to

NEW DIRECTIONS FOR YOUTH DEVELOPMENT • DOI: 10.1002/yd

promoting changes in thought, motivation, and behavior in adolescents is necessary in order to promote successful instruction for purpose. Given the need for such changes to occur, we next describe methods for life purpose instruction.

Purpose-driven discussions

Given Damon, Menon, and Bronk's definition of purpose, it is important to note that one must integrate three levels within oneself to reach a purposeful life: knowing what goal in life to pursue, having the motivation and desire to pursue such a goal, and participating in specific behaviors in order to attain the goal. Open discussions are essential to the promotion of positive purpose because these activities are likely to stimulate conversations about particular goals in life to pursue. Campbell found that an open classroom nurturing discussions about political issues increased civic knowledge for students.[32] Moreover, classroom openness to conflicting viewpoints increased students' appreciation for conflict in politics. In addition, by being active in the classroom, adolescents formed a civic identity and increased involvement in the political process. Similar to how a civic identity can be formed through active discussions, one would hope that open discussions surrounding purpose would promote purpose-driven identity formation. These discussions could help students increase their knowledge as to the various types of purpose that peers have and may help introduce them to paths through which they can pursue their own goals. Moreover, having discussions with peers who may or may not have similar purposes can help students think through their own rationale for pursuing specific purpose-driven activities within their own lives.

Experiential learning, service-learning, and goal-directed activities with like-minded peers

Purposeful motivation and action can be fostered through experiential and service-learning projects. Service-learning is a pedagogical method to connect school curriculum with service activities in the community. This type of learning also uses experiential reflections of the service to integrate course content into the individual's sense of self.[33] Service-learning is carried out to integrate motivation and behavior. Although most service-learning is used in character education, it can easily be used to promote purpose. For example, teachers can facilitate peer discussions that help students realize long-term goals. Once these goals have been identified, specific service projects can be undertaken within the community that assist students in the pursuit of their goals. Moreover, experiential reflection throughout the course can help integrate the course content into youth identities. This bridge between the classroom and the community can help students think beyond themselves, which promotes a component of purpose (contribution to the world).

Significance of promoting youth purpose

As already noted, a sense of purpose may be a key basis for the development of a variety of assets in adolescents. Positive purpose during adolescence can lead to prosocial behavior, moral commitment, high self-esteem, achievement, and physical and psychological well-being.[34] For instance, African American adolescents who were exposed to violence in the home were more resilient to negative social and psychological factors when they had a higher sense of purpose.[35] Erikson also reported positive outcomes of purpose: having purpose helped young people resolve issues surrounding identity.[36]

In addition, positive purpose promotes the well-being of others by a beyond-the-self focus. The beyond-the-self quality of purpose can help adolescents think beyond personal gains and help promote moral actions for the sake of others. Integrating instructional support for purpose in school settings can lead to self and societal well-being, as indicated by previous research.

Discussion

This review revealed that few formal educational programs for explicitly teaching purpose are documented in the research literature. Yet clearly the review has limitations. First, we chose to focus on reports in journal articles and based this on the traditional assumption that the most rigorous research will be reported in such publications. However, the interest in youth purpose has undergone a resurgence, and new areas of study often take time before their products appear in more established publications. Journal publications on youth purpose to date center on definitional matters and psychological correlates. Other publication venues, such as books and book chapters, may have provided insights into how purpose is taught. Second, the dearth of research on purpose instruction led us to review purpose-related constructs. However, the review only skims approaches to teach for character, civic engagement, and PYD because a more extensive coverage of these areas would be far beyond the scope of the article.

In spite of its limitations, this review reveals several important facets that could be examined for their usefulness and pioneered through in-school and out-of-school-time environments. First, educators and researchers will want to consider studying and then applying long-term approaches to purpose curricula that foster a sense of continuity rather than one-stop-lesson approaches. Single lessons are important but should consider adolescents' broader educational contexts. Attention should be given to cultural practices and features that support purpose because these connect to adolescents' lives beyond school. Understanding adolescents' lives may clue educators into their students' personal interests and concerns, and these should be discovered and fostered in conjunction with engaging youth in activities that serve the social good, thus encouraging a sense of ownership of participation and an authentic sense of engagement. Such activities might include service-learning, experiential learning focused on prosocial purpose, and purpose discussions that promote deep reflection. A second important feature of purpose education is to provide practically useful activities and concrete ways for youth to exercise their interests and goals. Youth are not passive recipients of purpose and need to perceive clear pathways and tools by which they can activate their goals. Finally, educators of purpose would do well to foster an awareness of the multiple sources of long-term and close personal support that are needed and exist in adolescents' lives and to bring this support to bear on adolescents' purpose development.

Notes

1. Damon, W., Menon, J., & Bronk, K. C. (2003). The development of purpose during adolescence. *Applied Developmental Science, 7*(3), 119–128.

2. Bronk, K. C. (2008). Humility among adolescent purpose exemplars. *Journal of Research on Character Education, 6*(1), 35–51.

3. Althof, W., & Berkowitz, M. W. (2006). Moral education and character education: Their relationship and roles in citizenship education. *Journal of Moral Education, 35*, 495–518.

4. White, K. J., Wagener, L. M., & Furrow, J. L. (2010). Purpose in adolescence, what am I here for? A qualitative examination on the expression, development and integration of purpose in at-risk and thriving male adolescents. *International Journal of Existential Psychology and Psychotherapy, 3*(1), 1–16.

5. Mariano, J. M. (2011). *An examination of how formal and informal educational contexts support purpose in adolescent girls.* Unpublished manuscript submitted for publication.

6. Pletcher, G. D. (2002, March). *In the thick of the fight: Service and learning in progressive era composition.* Paper presented at the annual meeting of the Conference on College Composition and Communication, Chicago, IL.

7. Mariano, J. M., Going, J., Schrock, K., & Sweeting, K. (2011). Youth purpose and perceived social supports among ethnic minority middle school girls. *Journal of Youth Studies, 14*(11), 921–938.

8. Cernik, H. C. (1968). Learning purposes of high school youth in relation to five destiny areas. *Character Potential: A Record of Research, 4*(3), 49–53; Glasson, M. C. (1968). The congress participants and their individual preparation. *Character Potential: A Record of Research, 4*(3), 5–8; Howell, M. (1973). Discovering a vision for your life; A sequential guidance program in a junior high school. *Character Potential: A Record of Research, 6*(2), 45–60; Mueller, N. J. (1973). The personality profile: Research and development. *Character Potential: A Record of Research, 6*(1), 32–37.

9. Glasson. (1968). P. 6.

10. Howell. (1973).

11. Kosine, N., Steger, M. F., & Duncan, S. (2008). Purpose-centered career development: A strengths-based approach to finding meaning and purpose in careers. *Professional School Counseling, 12*(2), 133–136.

12. Cohen, A. (1993). A new educational paradigm. *Phi Delta Kappan, 74*(10), 791–795; Nicklin, J. L. (1995, July 14). Education with a purpose. *Chronicle of Higher Education, 41*(44), A13–A14; Cohen, A., & Jordan, J. (1996). Audrey Cohen College System of Education: Purpose-centered education. In S. Stringfield, S. M. Ross, & L. Smith (Eds.), *Bold plans for school restructuring: The New American Schools designs* (pp. 25–52). Mahwah, NJ: Erlbaum.

13. Cohen. (1993).

14. Worthen, R., Johnson, B., Badore, N., & Bentley, M. (1973). Adolescent adjustment related to the purpose in life test. *Journal of Community Psychology, 1*(2), 209–211.

15. Mariano. (2011).

16. Mariano. (2011).

17. Hansell, S. (1983). Student commitment and purpose in a private secondary school. *Qualitative Sociology, 6*(2), 163–181.

18. Lickona, T. (1991). *Educating for character.* New York, NY: Bantam Books.

19. Berkowitz, M. W., & Bier, M. C. (2005). *What works in character education: A research-driven guide for educators.* Washington, DC: Character Education Partnership.

20. Berger, R. (2003). *An ethic of excellence: Building a culture of craftsmanship with students.* Portsmouth, NH: Heinemann.

21. Dymond, S., Renzaglia, A., & Chun, E. J. (2008). Elements of high school service learning programs. *Career Development for Exceptional Individuals, 31*, 37–47.

22. Leming, J. S. (2001). Integrating a structured ethical reflection curriculum into high school community service experiences: Impact on students' sociomoral development. *Adolescence, 36*, 33–45; Mayhew, M. J., & King, P. (2008). How curricular content and pedagogical strategies affect moral reasoning development in college students. *Journal of Moral Education, 37*, 17–40.

23. Lickona, T., Schaps, E., & Lewis, C. (2007). *CEP's eleven principles of effective character education.* Washington, DC: Character Education Partnership.

24. Feldman, L., Pasek, J., Romer, D., & Jamieson, K. H. (2007). Identifying best practices in civic education: Lessons from the Student Voices Program. *American Journal of Education, 114*, 75–100.

25. Branson, M. S. (1998). *The role of civic education.* Retrieved from http://new.civiced.org/programs/promote-civics

26. CIRCLE & Carnegie Corporation of New York. (2003). *The civic mission of schools.* New York, NY: Carnegie Corporation of New York.

27. Branson. (1998).

28. Branson. (1998).

29. Benson, P. L. (2003). Developmental assets and asset-building community: Conceptual and empirical foundations. In R. M. Lerner & P. L. Benson (Eds.), *Developmental assets and asset-building communities: Implications for research, policy, and practice* (pp. 19–43). Norwell, MA: Kluwer.

30. Eccles, J., & Gootman, J. A. (Eds.). (2002). *Community programs to promote youth development.* Washington, DC: National Academies Press.

31. Borden, L., & Serido, J. (2009). From program participant to engaged citizen: A developmental journey. *Journal of Community Psychology, 37*, 423–438.

32. Campbell, D. E. (2008). Voice in the classroom: How an open classroom climate fosters political engagement among adolescents. *Political Behavior, 30*, 437–454.

33. Dymond et al. (2008).

34. Damon et al. (2003).

35. DuRant, R. H., Cadenhead, C., Pendergrast, R. A., Slavens, G., & Linder, C. W. (1994). Factors associated with the use of violence among urban black adolescents. *American Journal of Public Health, 84*, 612–617.

36. Erikson, E. H. (1968). *Identity: Youth and crisis.* New York, NY: Norton.

SONIA ISSAC KOSHY *is an evaluation specialist with Thrive Foundation for Youth.*

JENNI MENON MARIANO *is an assistant professor of educational psychology and human development at the University of South Florida Sarasota-Manatee.*

*Researchers have argued that purpose supports
healthy adolescent development. This study shows
how youth purpose reinforces one aspect of healthy
development: identity formation.*

2

The role of purpose in life in healthy identity formation: A grounded model

Kendall Cotton Bronk

EDUCATORS OFTEN BEMOAN the challenge of motivating secondary education students to excel in the classroom. Why is it so difficult to get some adolescents to want to learn? More and more, researchers are connecting a lack of motivation in the classroom with a lack of purpose among the students. Students who do not know why they need to master academic material are not particularly motivated to do so, but students who know what they want out of life and see how what they are learning in class can help them achieve their goals are likely to be highly motivated in the classroom. Educators therefore should focus on inspiring and supporting a meaningful sense of purpose in the lives of their students.

Beyond serving as a critical source of motivation, a purpose in life may also serve as an important component of healthy identity formation; however, this possibility has gone largely unexamined. Although theoretical research has linked purpose to

NEW DIRECTIONS FOR YOUTH DEVELOPMENT, NO. 132, WINTER 2011 © WILEY PERIODICALS, INC.
Published online in Wiley Online Library (wileyonlinelibrary.com) • DOI: 10.1002/yd.426

healthy identity development, empirical work on the topic is lacking.

Erikson was one of the earliest scholars to suggest that under optimal conditions, both a purpose in life and a clear sense of identity develop during adolescence and emerging adulthood.[1] More contemporary researchers have empirically established that youth explore and commit to purposes at the same time as they explore and commit to identities.[2] Not only do purpose and identity develop at roughly the same time, but they also share a focus on personally meaningful beliefs and aims. However, despite their concomitant appearance in the life span and their shared focus, purpose and identity are distinct constructs.

Identity describes personally meaningful aims and beliefs as they pertain to a consistent sense of who one is and who one hopes to become. According to Erikson, establishing a sense of identity results in "inner unity."[3] As individuals navigate adolescence, they determine who they are separate from their family of origin and as members of a wider society. Adolescents develop a philosophy of life and strive to establish a coherent, nuanced sense of career, moral, ethnic, religious, political, and sexual identity.

Purpose describes an enduring, personally meaningful commitment to what one hopes to accomplish or work toward in life. Although more specific definitions of *purpose* have varied in the past, there appears to be a growing consensus among researchers that a purpose represents a stable and generalized intention to accomplish something that is at once meaningful to the self and leads to productive engagement with some aspect of the world beyond the self.[4]

This definition has three important dimensions. First, a purpose in life represents the thing that an individual is working toward in life. It is an intention to progress toward a personally meaningful ultimate aim.[5] Second, personal meaningfulness is evidenced by active engagement on the part of the individual who commits time, energy, knowledge, and resources to achieving his or her purpose in life. Finally, purpose features a central desire to act in the world beyond the self or in pursuit of a larger cause. Purpose and meaning in life share an intention to see one's life as guided by an overarching aim; however, purpose is distinct from meaning in that a primary motivation for purpose is to have an impact on causes or individuals beyond the self.[6] Because action in the broader world can be prosocial, antisocial, or neutral in nature, a purpose in life can take any of these forms. The study we report here is concerned with noble, or at least neutral, purposes.

In sum, *identity* refers to the development of one's sense of self, and *purpose* refers to the development of what one hopes to accomplish in life. Furthermore, research finds that although all adolescents undergo identity development, only a small fraction undergoes purpose development. Empirical studies reveal that only about 20 percent of adolescents develop a clear sense of purpose in life.[7] This is problematic given that purpose has been identified as an important aspect of healthy identity formation.[8]

Although purpose and identity are distinguishable constructs, Erikson suggested they work in tandem.[9] For example, finding a purpose can help individuals resolve their identity crises by offering a meaningful aim toward which they can direct time, energy, and effort. Furthermore, successfully resolving identity crises can result in the development of new assets, capabilities, or talents, such as initiative and efficacy, that are likely to facilitate the growth of purpose. One of the primary benefits of identifying a purpose during adolescence may be that doing so promotes a positive, efficacious sense of identity that can facilitate the transition to adulthood.[10]

While Erikson and others have proposed that identity and purpose are related constructs, little research has focused on the way they function together.[11] This represents an important gap in the research since purpose has been determined to play an important role in healthy identity development and research finds that only a small portion of youth exhibit signs of purpose in their lives.[12] This study was designed to clarify the nature of the relationship between purpose and identity.

NEW DIRECTIONS FOR YOUTH DEVELOPMENT • DOI: 10.1002/yd

Methods

Sample

In order to understand how purpose is related to identity development, this study relied on data from three waves of in-depth, case study–style interviews conducted with eight adolescent exemplars of purpose. At time 1, participants were between twelve and twenty-two years old. The author wishes to keep this as "of age" (mean age = 17.25; SD = 3.06). Interviews were conducted approximately two and a half years later and again two years after that. The sample was intentionally broad, including both adolescents and emerging adults, because this study sought to explore the range of ways in which developing a purpose in life may influence identity development. This age range roughly corresponds to the years in which identity formation is particularly central to human development. Participants were Caucasian (63 percent), African American (13 percent), Asian (13 percent), and Hispanic (13 percent) and balanced for gender (50 percent female).

A case study–style exemplar methodology was appropriate for this study for several reasons. First, purpose and identity are both multifaceted constructs, featuring intention, engagement, and motivational components, and a case study–style methodology allowed researchers to gather highly detailed data, which were required to clarify the developmental process of such complex constructs. Second, adolescent purpose exemplars were included because viewing a construct in its most intense form is often the clearest way of discerning what that construct looks like in practice.[13] Echoing this advantage of exemplar research, Aristotle noted in *Nicomachean Ethics*, "We approach the subject of practical wisdom by studying the persons to whom we attribute it."[14] Similarly, Maslow argued that if we want to learn about ultimate human potential, we should study highly functional and enlightened individuals.[15]

Nomination criteria used to qualify purpose exemplars were derived primarily from the definition of purpose. The adolescent purpose exemplars:

1. Demonstrated enduring commitments to personally meaningful, long-term aims
2. Were actively engaged in working toward their aims and had plans for continuing to do so in the future
3. Were committed to these aims largely because pursuing them allowed the youth to have a positive impact on the broader world, including groups of people, causes, and artistic endeavors

These criteria were shared with expert nominators, including youth practitioners in a variety of fields (for example, high school teachers, music teachers, and youth ministers), who used them to identify the exemplars.

The exemplars' purposes varied widely. Five of the eight youth were dedicated to social causes: raising money to build wells in Africa, supporting cancer research, curbing gun violence, promoting adolescent health, and preserving the environment. The other three youth were devoted to domain-specific aims: creating jazz music, promoting conservative political ideals, and serving God.

Data collection and analysis

The purpose exemplars were interviewed for approximately three hours every other year for five years using a semistructured, case study–style interview protocol. The youth purpose interview protocol, which asked participants about the things that mattered most to them, was administered at time 1.[16] Data from times 2 and 3 were collected using the revised youth purpose interview protocol, which asked participants what had changed regarding their commitments to, reasons behind, and involvement in the things that mattered most to them since the prior interview.[17] Participants reflected on their reasons for becoming and staying involved in their various areas of interest. They agreed to participate and, when appropriate, parents consented to having minors participate.

The grounded theory method, initially developed by Glaser and Strauss and elaborated on by Strauss and Corbin, provided the framework for this study.[18] This methodology is useful for inductively deriving rich theoretical understandings directly from the data. As such, findings presented in this study should be viewed in light of that aim.

Means of carrying out grounded theory research vary. This study employed the constant comparison method, which represents a process of continually redesigning the research in light of emerging codes, concepts, and relationships among the variables.[19] Members of the research team read through transcripts noting themes and patterns that emerged first within participants and later across them. These trends and patterns served as the basis for code generation. Emerging codes were applied to each transcript, and elaborations, refinements, and omissions were made as needed in order to ensure that the codes accurately described the data. Codes were then grouped into concepts, and concepts were linked to one another to develop a model of the way that purpose and identity develop.

Results

Purpose helped foster identity formation

The adolescent purpose exemplars pointed to a variety of experiences in which having established a meaningful purpose in life facilitated identity formation. In particular, having a purpose in life influenced the way the purpose exemplars viewed themselves with regard to the broader social world both in relation to the people they came into regular contact with and over time. Cote and Levine refer to these varied perspectives on self as individuals' social, personal, and ego identities, respectively. Purpose helped foster the development of both social and ego identities.[20]

First, through their purposeful commitments, the exemplars began to see how they fit into the broader world, and through this process they began to establish a social identity. For example, as a result of being involved in the American Cancer Society, the eighteen-year-old cancer researcher said, "You see sort of your place in the world. You see how you're not just lost in the sea of things, how you actually can contribute and how you can somehow affect someone else's life in any regard and I think that that's necessary. We're not isolated people." At age sixteen, the environmentalist said:

[Pursuing my environmental interests has allowed me to find] my place in the world. ... To have found where I feel like I'm doing something for the place that I live, which is my world. Feeling like this is where I'm supposed to be, this is the job I'm supposed to be performing, and I'm benefiting these people . . . in the work I do. I'm helping someone else because of the abilities that I have. ... There are things that I have to offer to this world.

Similarly, at twelve years of age, the well builder said, "The world is like a huge puzzle, and we have to try to figure out where our pieces fit. I figured out when I was six years old that I wanted to do something about the water crisis." In other words, establishing a purpose in life helped the well builder and the other exemplars better understand how they fit into the social world around them.

Second, having a purpose in life contributed to identity development, as adolescent purpose exemplars established an enduring sense of self, or an ego identity, rooted in their various purposes in life. *Ego identity* refers to a "vital sense of one's continuity and sameness."[21] Whereas a social identity refers to the one's place in the broader world, ego identity refers to a consistent sense of who one is and encompasses personality and beliefs. Evidence of the central role of purpose in the establishment of an ego identity surfaced in the exemplars' quotations. For example, at sixteen years of age, the religious exemplar identified herself by her purpose: "I'm a Christian, because I'm dedicated to doing what God wants me to do." The conservative politician also defined himself by his purpose: "I did learn that I am passionate [about conservative politics], and I'm starting to kinda come to terms with that, to kinda be like, 'You know what? This is just you.'"

The health advocate's purpose in life provided a consistent strand of self-understanding for her developing identity. In considering her future, she knew that whatever she did, her life would revolve around her purpose: "It's becoming increasingly important to me to figure out my life trajectory. I've had direction from early on in terms of [knowing that I wanted to work on health-related issues], but there are a lot of different things you could do within that sphere." In other words, having a purpose in life provided a key sense of direction for her identity development. In sum, having a clear purpose helped the exemplars establish both social and ego identities.

Identity formation reinforced purposeful commitments

As the adolescents established identities based on their purposeful commitments, their identities reinforced their purposeful commitments. In other words, purpose led to identity development, and identity development reinforced commitments to purpose. As a result of establishing an identity based on their purposes in life, people close to the exemplars began to identify the exemplars by their purposes. These interactions with others influenced the purpose exemplars' personal identity development.[22] For instance, at eighteen years of age, the health advocate noted, "Most people can't have a conversation with me without [health-related] issues bubbling up to the surface, so I think it's very much a part of how I see things and how I frame things and what I think will work and what I don't think will work." Her purposeful commitment influenced the way others saw her, and this helped her establish a personal identity.

Having others identify the exemplars with their purposes reinforced the exemplars' commitments to purpose. In this way, establishing a personal identity helped solidify the adolescents' purposeful commitments.[23] For example, at twenty years of age, the gun control advocate identified himself as a "security guru" to his friends and colleagues, and at sixteen the environmentalist embraced the "tree hugger" label her friends gave her: "Environmental work is a big, big part of my life. … We're the tree huggers at school. We're the only environmental people who stand out, really, I guess. So we get called 'tree hugger' all the time." Recognizing that others associated her with her environmental work led her to invest further in this personally meaningful effort.

Similarly, when the musician began to take on a musical identity at eighteen years of age, he became more committed to pursuing his musical interests. Reflecting on the decision of which college to attend, an engineering school or a music school, he said:

The reason I went toward jazz is I was, compared to everybody else, I was special in jazz. ... A lot of people can get A's in calculus and could be engineers. ... [But] I didn't know anybody else who played jazz piano and took it as seriously as I did. ... I identified with it. "Oh, who's that guy?" "Oh, that's P. He plays jazz piano." I didn't get, "Oh that's P, he's good at math."

Being a musician allowed this young man to be interesting and eccentric, and he valued that sense of self: "I had always thought of music very seriously, and I always thought of academics very seriously, but academics was a more conventional thing. Lots of people were doing that. And that's one of the reasons I went away from it, because it was normal." Becoming a musician offered an appealing alternative identity and led him to make decisions that deepened his commitment to music. In this way, identity formation supported and even deepened his purpose commitment. As a result of interactions with those close to them, the exemplars identified themselves by their purposes, and this served to reinforce their commitments to purpose.

Purpose and identity as overlapping constructs

Finally, in addition to being reinforcing constructs, purpose and identity were largely overlapping constructs in the lives of adolescent purpose exemplars. Individuals felt that who they were was synonymous with what they hoped to accomplish. For instance, at twenty years of age, the health advocate said, "I never feel like I've got to go spend some time on me, now, and go do something for me. It's like the stuff that I do with other people is for me too, so there's not that dichotomy, and not that need to go disconnect from it all the time, because I feel like it's so much a part of me." Just as the health advocate identified herself by her purposeful commitments, so too did the musician: "I identified with [jazz]. ... I've found an identity. I've found something I enjoy doing. I have a love." At sixteen years old, the environmentalist described herself through her purpose: "[Recycling] is one of those things that's become habit to me. ... [Everyone knows] that I'm a person who recycles." When asked to describe what kind of person he was, the gun control advocate said, "[I'm someone who has] a really strong commitment to doing something to improve this world. ... I've been involved for many years in activism against gun violence." The adolescent purpose exemplars described who they were in large part by citing their various purposes in life.

Discussion

This study yielded at least three important and related findings with regard to the adolescent purpose exemplars:

1. The development of purpose facilitated identity formation.
2. Identity development reinforced the exemplars' commitments to purposes.
3. Purpose and identity appeared to be largely overlapping constructs.

As Erikson and others have proposed, establishing a purpose in life helped the exemplars establish a sense of identity.[24] Identity formation occurs largely as a result of being engaged in the environment in a meaningful way.[25] Findings from this study confirm that the exemplars' purposes helped them understand their place in the broader social world and over time. These findings suggest that one way that purpose may contribute to positive developmental outcomes such as happiness, resiliency, subjective well-being, psychological well-being, positive affect, and life satisfaction is through its role as an identity-related resource.[26] The identity capital model suggests that tangible and intangible resources assist optimal identity formation and individualization.[27] Committing to a purpose in life may serve as an important intangible, identity-related resource, as finding a sense of purpose for their lives offered the exemplars a direction toward which to dedicate their energy and focus. In this way, having a purpose in life helped the exemplars develop in positive ways.

Second, not only did the development of purpose facilitate identity formation, but identity formation also supported the ongoing development of purpose. As Erikson noted, the development of purpose appears to precede the development of identity, so it is not surprising that this study found that identity formation did not spur purpose development but instead supported its ongoing development.[28] Bem's self-perception theory suggests that individuals infer their attitudes in part by observing their own behavior.[29] It seems likely that the exemplars' continued involvement led them to infer a deep connection to the activities in which they were involved. Individuals close to the exemplars confirmed this connection by identifying these young people with their involvement. In this way, the exemplars' developing sense of identity served to deepen their commitment to their purposeful interests.

Finally, the study proposed a model where purpose and identity not only reinforce one another but are also closely aligned. The model of purpose and identity may mirror the model of moral identity, in which for moral exemplars an individual's sense of self and moral concerns are closely aligned.[30] This model of moral identity further finds that when an individual's sense of self and his or her moral concerns are less well aligned, a weaker moral identity is evident. It seems likely that the same holds for purpose and identity. Research finds that youth can be divided into one of three categories: those who meet all the criteria for purpose, those who meet some of the criteria for purpose, and those who meet none of the criteria for purpose.[31] It seems logical that youth who meet only some of the criteria for purpose would demonstrate poorer alignment between their sense of self and their emerging sense of purpose, as these youth presumably do not see their ultimate aims as central to who they are. Similarly, it seems logical that youth who do not demonstrate any signs of purpose are unlikely to have a sense of self that is not aligned at all with their ultimate aims, as they have not committed to any enduring aims. Empirical research is needed to test these two latter alternatives.

In sum, educators and policymakers alike should focus on supporting the development of purpose among young people for a variety of reasons. As young people commit to a purpose in life, they are likely to become more motivated students. Beyond this, as this study finds, fostering a sense of purpose among students is also likely to facilitate identity formation. By helping young people identify and foster the skills needed to work toward issues that inspire them, parents, educators, and others concerned about young people's welfare will also be helping them develop a positive identity, which is key to psychological well-being.

Notes

1. Erikson, E. H. (1968). *Identity: Youth and crisis*. New York, NY: Norton.
2. Burrow, A. L., O'Dell, A., & Hill, P. (2010). Profiles of a developmental asset: Youth purpose as a context for hope and well-being. *Journal of Youth and Adolescence, 39*, 1265–1273.
3. Erikson. (1968). P. 92.
4. Damon, W., Menon, J., & Bronk, K. C. (2003). The development of purpose during adolescence. *Applied Developmental Science, 7*(3), 119–128.
5. Emmons, R. A. (1999). *The psychology of ultimate concerns: Motivation and spirituality in personality*. New York, NY: Guilford Press.
6. Steger, M. F., Oishi, S., & Kashdan, T. B. (2009). Meaning in life across the life span: Levels and correlates of meaning in life from adolescence to older adulthood. *Journal of Positive Psychology, 4*, 43–52.
7. Damon, W. (2008). *The path to purpose: Helping children find their calling in life*. New York, NY: Free Press; Moran, S. (2009). Purpose: Giftedness in intrapersonal intelligence. *High Ability Studies, 20*(2), 143–159; Bronk, K. C., Finch, W. H., & Talib, T. (2010). Purpose in life among high ability adolescents. *High Ability Studies, 21*(2), 133–145.
8. Erikson. (1968); Damon. (2008).
9. Erikson. (1968). P. 16.
10. Burrow et al. (2010).

11. Erikson. (1968); for example: Damon. (2008); Bronk et al. (2010); Moran. (2009).

12. Erikson. (1968); for example: Damon. (2008); Moran. (2009); Bronk et al. (2010).

13. Colby, A., & Damon, W. (1992). *Some do care: Contemporary lives of moral commitment.* New York, NY: Free Press.

14. Aristotle. (1962). *Nicomachean ethics.* Upper Saddle River, NJ: Prentice Hall.

15. Maslow, A. (1971). *The farther reaches of human nature.* New York, NY: Viking Press.

16. Bronk, K. C., Menon, J., & Damon, W. (2004). *Youth purpose interview.* Unpublished instrument. Stanford, CA: Stanford Center on Adolescence.

17. Andrews, M. C., Bundick, M. J., Jones, A., Bronk, K. C., Mariano, J. M., & Damon, W. (2006). *Youth purpose interview, version 2006.* Unpublished instrument. Stanford, CA: Stanford Center on Adolescence.

18. Glaser, B. G., & Strauss, A. J. (1967). *The discovery of grounded theory: Strategies for qualitative research.* Chicago, IL: Aldine; Strauss, A. J., & Corbin, J. (1998). *Basics of qualitative research: Techniques and procedures for developing grounded theory* (2nd ed.). Thousand Oaks, CA: Sage.

19. Glaser, B. G. (1965). The constant comparative method of qualitative analysis. *Social Problems, 12,* 436–445.

20. Cote, J. E., & Levine, C. G. (2002). *Identity formation, agency, and culture: A social psychological synthesis.* Mahwah, NJ: Erlbaum.

21. Cote & Levine. (2002). P. 182.

22. Cote & Levine. (2002).

23. Cote & Levine. (2002).

24. Erikson. (1968); for example: Damon. (2008); Moran. (2009); Cote & Levine. (2002).

25. Erikson, E. H. (1958). *Young man Luther: A study in psychoanalysis and history.* New York, NY: Norton; Erikson, E. H. (1969). *Gandhi's truth: On the origins of militant nonviolence.* New York, NY: Norton.

26. Benard, B. (1991). *Fostering resiliency in kids: Protective factors in the family, school and community.* San Francisco, CA: Western Regional Center for Drug Free Schools and Communities, Far West Laboratory; Bronk, K. C., Hill, P., Lapsley, D. K., Talib, T., & Finch, H. (2009). Purpose, hope, and life satisfaction in three age groups. *Journal of Positive Psychology, 4*(6), 500–510; French, S., & Joseph, S. (1999). Religiosity and its association with happiness, purpose in life, and self-actualization. *Mental Health, Religion, and Culture, 2,* 117–120; Keyes, C.L.M., Shmotkin, D., & Ryff, C. D. (2002). Optimizing well-being: The empirical encounter of two traditions. *Journal of Personality and Social Psychology, 82*(6), 1007–1022; King, L. A., Hicks, J. A., Krull, J., & Del Gaiso, A. K. (2006). Positive affect and the experience of meaning in life. *Journal of Personality and Social Psychology, 90,* 179–196; Masten, A. S., & Reed, M.G.J. (2002). Resilience in development. In C. R. Snyder & S. J. Lopez (Eds.), *Handbook of positive psychology* (pp. 74–88). New York, NY: Oxford University Press; Ryff, C. D., & Keyes, C.L.M. (1995). The structure of psychological well-being revisited. *Journal of Personality and Social Psychology, 69*(4),

719–727; Seligman, M.E.P. (2002). *Authentic happiness: Using the new positive psychology to realize your potential for lasting fulfillment.* New York, NY: Free Press.

27. Cote, J. E. (2002). The role of identity capital in the transition to adulthood: The individualization thesis examined. *Journal of Youth Studies, 5*(2), 117–134; Cote & Levine. (2002).

28. Erikson. (1968).

29. Bem, D. (1972). Self-perception theory. In L. Berkowitz (Ed.), *Advances in experimental social psychology* (Vol. 6, pp. 1–62). Orlando, FL: Academic Press; Bem, D. (1967). Self-perception: An alternative interpretation of cognitive dissonance phenomena *Psychological Review, 74, 183 200.*

30. Blasi, A. (1984). Moral identity: Its role in moral functioning. In W. M. Kurtines & J. L. Gewirtz (Eds.), *Morality, moral behavior, and moral development* (pp. 129–139). Hoboken, NJ: Wiley.

31. Bronk et al. (2010); Bronk, K. C., & Finch, W. H. (2010). Adolescent characteristics by type of long-term aim in life. *Applied Developmental Science, 14*(1), 1–10; Bronk, K. C. (2008). Humility among adolescent purpose exemplars. *Journal of Research on Character Education, 6*(1), 35–51.

KENDALL COTTON BRONK *is an assistant professor of educational psychology at Ball State University.*

Activities at school and in the community, along with work, are important to support the development of a strong sense of purpose.

3

Supporting a strong sense of purpose: Lessons from a rural community

Devora Shamah

FINDING ONE'S PLACE in the world is a developmental process that spans the life course.[1] In adolescence, individuals are just beginning to develop their sense of purpose, or "a stable and generalized intention to accomplish something that is at once meaningful to the self and of consequence to the world beyond the self."[2] Understanding the processes by which youth develop a strong sense of purpose is critical for supporting youth. Unlike measures of academic achievement and social competence, sense of purpose provides insight into the identity work that adolescents have or have

This study was supported by an American Fellowship from the American Association of University Women; a Stanford Center on Adolescence Youth Purpose Research Award supported by the John Templeton Foundation and the Thrive Foundation for Youth; and the Sustainable Rural Communities Initiative at Oregon State University, College of Health and Human Sciences at Oregon State University, and Department of Human Development and Family Studies at Oregon State University.

not achieved. Understanding youth development with respect to sense of purpose may help us think about ways to position youth to navigate the transition to adulthood successfully.

This article examines sense of purpose among youth living in one county in rural Oregon. We focus on a rural context in part because the social processes important to development are more visible in small communities, offering an ideal setting for an initial examination of processes surrounding development of a sense of purpose.[3] In addition, the focus on rural youth is in response to the need to better understand the strengths of rural places (for example, strong intergenerational relationships, small schools, and productive work opportunities) in the face of global changes that are dramatically altering the social structure of rural communities across the United States.[4] This study used a symbolic interactionist perspective paired with survey and ethnographic strategies to examine the development of a sense of purpose.[5] The broader study was guided by this question: How do experiences within place shape the development of sense of purpose among rural youth? Findings suggest an important interplay of family, school, and community processes. Our focus is on the role of out-of-school activities, including sports participation and work.

Rural places in the United States differ in terms of the robustness of their economies, local histories, and ways in which they prepare young people for adulthood.[6] Despite these differences, most rural places share similarities. High schools are generally small, and a lack of anonymity dominates small town culture.[7] In a rural place, everywhere young people go, they generally run into someone who has known them for their whole life or is friends with their parents, which can make it difficult for them to try on new identities as part of identity development.[8] Youth in small towns commonly tell stories of how their parents hear about trouble they got into at school before they get home. The economic pressures that push them to leave their towns to attend college or find work after high school graduation also means leaving the fishbowl of small town life.[9] Often it is in these new places that rural youth continue their identity work of discovering who they are as individuals, distinct from their families.

This almost inevitable separation from the small communities where youth grew up may make sense of purpose even more important to the development of adolescents who come of age in rural places. A strong sense of purpose will likely help them negotiate the challenges of navigating a new place as they move into college and work and establish who they are.[10] Just as developing a strong sense of purpose may play a unique role for rural adolescents, the processes that contribute to developing a strong sense of purpose may be unique as well. Although processes may differ for rural youth and their urban and suburban peers, these processes offer insight into how to better support all adolescents in developing a strong sense of purpose that will serve them well as they move into adulthood.

Out-of-school activities have been linked to academic success and positive developmental pathways.[11] Much of this research has been done in urban and suburban contexts, though some has shown similar results in rural communities.[12] In this study, it was expected that out-of-school activities and sports participation would provide opportunities to develop a strong sense of purpose in youth. Work was also expected to play a role, especially in light of the strong value many rural communities place on it.[13] Work, like other out-of-school activities, is complex, and not all work experiences are similar. Within this community, however, it was expected that many teenagers would have access to meaningful work experiences and that in combination with out-of-school activities, these experiences would contribute to sense of purpose.[14]

These data were collected and analyzed using a symbolic interactionist perspective.[15] Symbolic interaction proposes that youth construct their identity through interactions with their environment, families, and communities. Sense-of-purpose development is part of identity development, and this study expected youth to construct and develop a sense of purpose through these interactions as well.

Methods

This article draws on a case study of Wallowa County, Oregon. Wallowa County, with a population of seven thousand, is known for graduating youth who are successful based on indicators such as high school graduation, truancy rates, and risky behaviors.[16] This community was chosen to provide insight into the processes of sense-of-purpose development among youth who are generally doing well and are supported by their community. High-school-aged youth were surveyed in their schools. Of the 313 students enrolled, 270 completed surveys, an 87 percent response rate. The survey included a sense-of-purpose scale adapted from Hutzell and Finck, with questions about participants' aspirations and demographic information.[17]

From the survey responses, a random sample was drawn from three groups of students identified using a latent class analysis. From this sample, twenty juniors and seniors participated in a series of interviews about their family, school, sense of purpose, and plans for the future. In addition, they took researchers on a community tour. Ethnographic data were coded using a categorical analysis to find patterns within groups that were identified based on original sense-of-purpose scores from the survey. Together, ethnographic and survey data provided insight into the development of sense of purpose and how these youth perceived their school, family, and community.

Results

The survey provided a general picture of the types of activities that youth in the county participated in, along with a general understanding of a typical young person in the county in terms of demographics, sense of purpose, aspirations, and desire to live in a rural place as an adult. The findings from the interview participants provided greater insight into kinds of activities that might be important for the development of sense of purpose.

Survey Findings

The survey participants were representative of the county where they live, which is predominantly white. Eighty-eight percent of the participants identified as white, 54 percent identified as male, and they averaged fifteen and a half years old. On average they had lived in the county for eleven years. The mean score on sense of purpose was 67.87, with a possible range of 23 to 92 points. Based on the methodology that Hutzell and Finck used, youth were divided into three groups using this mean score: high (75–91 points), average (61–74 points), and low sense of purpose (32–60 points).[18] These groups represent the high, low, and average sense-of-purpose groups for the community.

About 70 percent of the survey participants reported participating in school sports, and just under half reported participating in other school activities (46 percent). Only forty-five in the survey (17 percent) reported not participating in any sports or school activities. When participation patterns are considered in terms of sense-of-purpose group membership, about one-third (32.8 percent) of youth in the low sense-of-purpose group do not report participating in any school or sports activities.

Correlations were run with the full survey sample using sense-of-purpose scores and the following variables: parent education level, family years in the county; youth's years in the county; youth's desire to live in a rural place (a proxy for perceptions of rural living); family involvement with ranching, timber, or farming; church attendance; and participation in 4-H, Future Farmers of America (FFA), or school sports. All the variables were significantly correlated with sense-of-purpose group membership except church attendance and family years in the county. The strongest correlations were with participation in sports ($r = .32$, $p < .001$) and the desire to live in a rural place ($r = .35$, $p < .001$).

Sense-of-purpose groups

Youth who scored in the high sense-of-purpose group were generally good students who participated in a wide range of school activities and worked at least during the summer. Their families varied in structure, though among interview participants, all youth lived with two parents. Their parents also varied greatly in terms of income, with some families earning high incomes for the county and others living well below the poverty line and cobbling together several jobs to make a living. Parents also varied in their education level within the high sense-of-purpose interview participants. With the exception of one family, each youth had at least one parent with a bachelor's degree.

Among youth who scored low on sense of purpose, many were poor students. Some had already left public school for alternative school, and some were straight A students. Many participated in sports, but their overall participation was lower as a group than their peers who scored higher on sense of purpose. Their families also varied in structure, and within the interview participants' families, parents held high school diplomas or some college credits, but none held a bachelor's degree.

Out-of-school activities

The survey indicated the prevalence of participating in sports or other out-of-school activities. Interview participants provided insight into why these activities were important. Of the twenty in the group, six were in the high sense-of-purpose group, four were in the low sense-of-purpose group, and the remaining ten youth were in the middle. All of the high sense-of-purpose youth had participated in out-of-school activities. Most had played sports, and several had participated in FFA, drama, or school leadership. These youth often moved easily between sports and other activities like drama. Despite our expectations, three of the four youth with a low sense of purpose had been involved in sports for at least one season and were participating in other activities such as drama or clubs (this was not true of all the youth with a low sense of purpose among the survey sample, in part because some of them were much less engaged in school, if engaged at all).

Youth recognized that their coaches valued teamwork. They generally practiced daily during their sports seasons. Many youth felt the same way about sports, as this high sense-of-purpose youth described: "Sports is a huge part of my life." Sports also served as a way to introduce youth to the community, as observed by a low sense-of-purpose youth: "Because of sports everyone knows everyone." Despite the importance of sports and out-of-school activities in this community, work and community activities appear to play an equal or perhaps greater role in the development of sense of purpose among youth.

Community activities and work

The community in this study afforded youth remarkable opportunities to participate in a community orchestra, a literary organization that frequently offered literary workshops, church youth groups, and a cooperative ski slope. These activities differed from school-sponsored activities because they were not only for youth. In these activities, young people interacted with a wide spectrum of adults, and in a county where only 20.3 percent of the adults over twenty-five years old have a bachelor's degree or higher, these were often places to meet adults who were more educated or had jobs that were different from those held by their parents and teachers.

Youth who scored in the high and average sense-of-purpose groups participated in community activities. With the exception of occasional participation in church youth groups with friends, none of the low sense-of-purpose interview participants were involved in these activities. Of the sixty-seven survey participants with low sense-of-purpose scores, about a third reported going to church, and only seven reported participating in activities outside school. According to interview participants, this was not because they did not feel invited or lacked access (all were asked directly about access and all were emphatic that they were welcome to join any activities or groups in the community), but rather because their time beyond school and school activities was dominated by family responsibilities or activities such as family gatherings, babysitting, or hunting trips. In contrast to their peers in the high sense-of-purpose group, the youth within the low sense-of-purpose group centered their activity participation on school. As one youth explained when asked about participating in activities outside school, "Most of the stuff I do is at school, and out-of-school stuff is for school."

Work is valued in many rural communities.[19] Although only 77.8 percent of youth in the survey reported having a job, every interview participant had some work experience. These experiences varied from babysitting for family friends, to cleaning cabins in the summer as part of the tourist industry, to working in a restaurant or moving irrigation pipes for the area's farmers. The jobs held by high sense-of-purpose youth offered responsibility and opportunities to interact with older community members. Three high sense-of-purpose youth did ranch work, one apprenticed in the family business, one worked for a local tourist attraction, and one worked with her parents when needed. It was not necessarily the work itself that these youth enjoyed, but the relationships they had with the people they worked for and the developmental benefits of work. As one youth said, "I liked working with my grandpa. He was pretty cool, old, and full of lots of wisdom." Typically the work that young people in this group did provided opportunities to develop both skills and relationships. Moreover, these youth were characterized not only by the type of work and activities they participated in, but also by the ways they made sense of their experiences. As a group, they spoke positively of school and community activities despite the work it took to balance their commitments.

Low sense-of-purpose youth tended to work at jobs that differed from those of their high sense-of-purpose peers. They held low-wage jobs that lacked regular hours and had little status, such as babysitting informally for friends and family, cleaning hotels, or fast food service work. One youth said of a cleaning job, "I'd never recommend it, ever. It was horrible, I think, because of the lady in charge." These youth did enjoy some of their jobs, though they commented that much of their pay was eaten up in gas money driving to tourist jobs away from town at the far end of the lake. These jobs did not carry with them the same long-term responsibility and respect as jobs held by high sense-of-purpose youth (for example, ranch work, contact with the public for tourist activities, full apprenticeships). Low sense-of-purpose youth lacked the relationships with their employers that high sense-of-purpose youth recognized and valued.

Most youth in the middle sense-of-purpose group had jobs that were similar to those held by their peers in the high sense-of-purpose group. They did ranch work or worked in tourist positions where they were interacting with the public as ticket takers or wait staff. Like their high sense-of-purpose counterparts, they took advantage of the intergenerational relationships they developed and embraced the responsibility they were given. Four youth had cleaning jobs that were far more similar to their peers in the low sense-of-purpose group. And like their peers, they complained about these jobs, especially the low pay.

Discussion

Overall, this analysis found that the activities youth participated in during school, outside school, and through work mattered for the development of a sense of purpose. Work activities that provided opportunities for responsibility and some decision making and activities that happened in the community seemed especially to support developing a strong sense of purpose during high school.

Out-of-school activities

Sports participation was clearly important for many of these youth and their identity development. Sports can be a forum where youth learn about having a purpose beyond themselves, and the participating students spoke highly of their coaches and the way their teams played for the team's gain rather than for personal glory. For some of them, this was the first time they observed sense of purpose on a small scale. A win, or playing well as a team, may become a central sense of purpose for all the team members and may guide some of their decisions. Modeling sense of purpose on the playing field may support youth as they ponder their purpose in the broader context of their communities and beyond. Of course, not every youth is an athlete or enjoys sports. Those in the high and middle sense-of-purpose groups also found niches in drama, FFA, and other school activities. All of these activities appear to have played a supporting role in their sense-of-purpose development. This supports other work that shows the benefits of out-of-school activities and may not be a rural phenomenon.[20]

Activities in the community beyond school seemed to make a difference for youth who scored high on sense of purpose. Some of these young people were active in their churches, a place linked with sense of purpose. Others played in the community orchestra or participated in workshops or volunteer work. These activities, coupled with meaningful work experiences, exposed youth to a wider spectrum of adults. These findings suggest that this exposure supports youth in developing a sense of purpose in ways that those scoring in the low group did not. Because activity participation and work happen within school and community contexts, future research should attempt to tease out the relationship between family influences and activity participation and determine if this is unique to youth living in rural areas.

Work

Paid work is a developmental experience that youth in the interviewed group shared, but like other research on work, the results showed that not all paid work is equal in the experiences it provides for youth.[21] Youth were doing everything from ranch work to cleaning for the tourist industry. Productive labor, or jobs that provided responsibility and clear skill building, support youth achievement. These jobs were held by high sense-of-purpose youth. Jobs such as house cleaning, babysitting, and fast food restaurant work do not build skills and tend to be more rigid, although there are exceptions, where a good manager can make any job a skill-building experience for youth, as Damon illustrated in *A Path to Purpose*.[22] In general, however, these types of jobs do not contribute to youth's development. Moreover, work can be detrimental to academic success, especially for students who attempt to work over twenty hours a week during the school year.[23] Among interview participants, most of the high sense-of-purpose youth were working over the summer but then focused on school activities and sports during the school year. The low sense-of-purpose youth followed a similar pattern, with babysitting being their primary work during the school year. Some youth in the middle were working more hours during the school year, but the study did not examine the influence of work hours on their development of sense of purpose.

Schools as buffer

This study revealed the powerful role that schools play in supporting youth in rural places. Of the four low sense-of-purpose interview participants at the time of the study, none had entered the juvenile justice system, all were still connected to school, and two were excellent students. Although these youth reported having less-than-optimal relationships with some of their peers and school staff, school had nevertheless engaged them. Researchers observed that every interview participant had a strong relationship with at least one adult in their school. This study, of course, was limited by the students who chose to participate, and there were likely youth no longer engaged with school who were not represented. For the low sense-of-purpose youth interviewed, however, school, and especially school activities, including sports and drama, were crucial in keeping them engaged with their peers.

This study points to the need to assess youth beyond mere academic measures of success to better prepare them for adulthood. The low sense-of-purpose group included youth who were successful based on their academic achievements and school engagement. Their low sense of purpose revealed their challenges with identity development that may lead to difficulty as they start to navigate adulthood in their communities. Particularly in rural communities where schools are generally small, there is an opportunity to encourage youth participation in community activities and connect youth with meaningful work opportunities that support the development of a sense of purpose.

Implications

Out-of-school activities of all kinds appear to support the development of a sense of purpose for the youth in this study. As a case study conducted in a rural county, the findings here may or may not extend to urban and suburban youth. That said, these findings support other work that has shown the value of out-of-school activities and productive work.[24] In larger places, community-based activities may not have the same importance as they do in small communities.

For teachers and community members, this means creating a wealth of ways for young people to explore their identities and experience being part of something beyond themselves. Providing additional alternatives to sports clubs is crucial and will continue to require the help of communities and volunteers as school budgets across the country are being cut. Young people who struggle with school have an additional challenge of connecting with peers and adults who value them outside school. Community-based music programs, gaming clubs, and apprenticeships can provide places for youth to feel valued and observe adults with a sense of purpose, as well as provide space for them to solidify their goals and figure out how those goals matter beyond themselves. Engaging in service-learning, other meaningful work, or other community activities that provide intergenerational interactions was essential to developing sense of purpose for the youth in this study.

Although mentors are important, the youth in this study described being exposed to a variety of adults who could model sense of purpose and encourage them to pursue their dreams. If schools intentionally evaluated purpose by using surveys or talking to students about purpose and assigned a school staff member to help students without a strong sense of purpose find meaningful work and service opportunities, many of these young people might strengthen their sense of purpose before heading out on their own.

Rural communities are well positioned to engage in this work because rural schools often are the center of the community.[25] A culture of community obligation often exists in rural places, but only some participants had engaged in that value, while others were more centered on school and family life.[26] Schools can be places that reinforce the value of contributing to the community through traditional activities, service-learning, and connections to the community. Perhaps all communities can learn from rural schools and seek innovative ways to provide a range of activities to engage all youth, from athletes to artists.

Although this study cannot definitively determine the interplay between sense of purpose and activities and work participation, it suggests that promoting engagement in both school and community activities, as well as meaningful work, would benefit rural youth—and perhaps all youth—in building the strong sense of purpose they need to carry them through the challenges of moving into adulthood.

Notes

1. Damon, W. (2008). *The path to purpose: Helping our children find their calling in life.* New York, NY: Free Press; Damon, W., Menon, J., & Bronk, K. C. (2003). The development of purpose during adolescence. *Applied Developmental Science, 7*(3), 119–128; Frankl, V. E. (1992/1959). *Man's search for meaning: An introduction to logotherapy* (4th ed.). Boston, MA: Beacon Press.

2. Damon et al. (2003). P. 121.

3. Colocousis, C. R., & Duncan, C. M. (2008). Rural communities: Good for studying neighborhood effects and social mobility. *Perspectives: On Poverty, Policy, and Place, 5*, 12–14.

4. Hamilton, L. C., Hamilton, L. R., Duncan, C. M., & Colocousis, C. R. (2008). Place matters: Challenges and opportunities in four rural Americas. Durham, NH: Carsey Institute. Retrieved from http://www.carseyinstitute .unh.edu/CarseySearch/search.php?id=98

5. Blumer, H. (1969). *Symbolic interactionism: Perspective and method.* Upper Saddle River, NJ: Prentice Hall; Mead, G. H. (1934). *Mind, self, and society: From the standpoint of a social behaviorist.* Chicago, IL: University of Chicago Press.

6. Hamilton, L. C., Hamilton, L. R., Duncan, C. M., & Colocousis, C. R. (2008); Duncan, C. M. (1999). *Worlds apart: Why poverty persists in rural America.* New Haven, CT: Yale University Press; Elder, G. H., Jr., & Conger, R. D. (2000). *Children of the land: Adversity and success in rural America.* Chicago, IL: University of Chicago Press; Salamon, S. (2003). *Newcomers to old towns: Suburbanization of the heartland.* Chicago, IL: University of Chicago Press.

7. Lyson, T. A. (2005). The importance of schools to rural community viability. In L. J. Beaulieu & R. Gibbs (Eds.), *The role of education: Promoting the economic and social vitality of rural America* (pp. 23–27). Mississippi State,

Mississippi. The address of the law center is Mississippi State, MS: Southern Rural Development Center. Retrieved from http://srdc.msstate.edu/publications/other/special/2005_01_roleofedu.pdf.

8. Hektner, J. M. (1995). When moving up implies moving out: Rural adolescent conflict in the transition to adulthood. *Journal of Research in Rural Education, 11*(1), 3–14.

9. Corbett, M. (2007). *Learning to leave: The irony of schooling in a coastal community.* Halifax, Canada: Fernwood Publishing; Hektner. (1995).

10. Damon. (2008).

11. Hansen, D. M., Larson, R. W., & Dworkin, J. B. (2003). What adolescents learn in organized youth activities: A survey of self reported developmental experiences. *Journal of Research on Adolescence, 13*(1), 25–55.

12. Elder & Conger. (2000).

13. Elder & Conger. (2000); Childress, H. (2000). *Landscapes of betrayal, landscapes of joy: Curtisville in the lives of its teenagers.* Albany: State University of New York Press; Monahan, K. C., Lee, J. M., & Steinberg, L. (2011). Revisiting the impact of part-time work on adolescent adjustment: Distinguishing between selection and socialization using propensity score matching. *Child Development, 82*(1), 96–112.

14. Damon. (2008); Yeager, D. S., & Bundick, M. J. (2009). The role of purposeful work goals in promoting meaning in life and in schoolwork during adolescence. *Journal of Adolescent Research, 24*(4), 423–452.

15. Blumer. (1969); Mead. (1934).

16. Temple, W. (2005) *Oregon benchmarks county data book.* Salem: Oregon Progress Board.

17. Hutzell, R. R., & Finck, W. C. (1994). Adapting the life purpose questionnaire for use in adolescent populations. *International Forum for Logotherapy, 17,* 42–46.

18. Hutzell & Finck. (1994).

19. Elder & Conger. (2000).

20. Hansen et al. (2003).

21. Childress. (2000); Elder & Conger. (2000); Williams, T. M., & Kornblum, W. (1985). *Growing up poor.* Lexington, MA: Lexington Books.

22. Damon. (2008).

23. Monahan et al. (2011).

24. Hansen et al. (2003); Childress. (2000).

25. Lyson. (2005).

26. Elder & Conger. (2000).

DEVORA SHAMAH *is a researcher at Gateway to College National Network.*

*Make Your Work Matter is a new, brief interven-
tion designed to help adolescents explore, discover,
and enact a sense of purpose in their early career
development.*

4
▬▬▬

Make Your Work Matter:
Development and pilot evaluation of
a purpose-centered career education
intervention

*Bryan J. Dik, Michael F. Steger,
Amanda Gibson, William Peisner*

INITIATING AND FOSTERING a sense of purpose has substantial developmental importance for adolescents.[1] There has been uniform
agreement that purpose is desirable, but little agreement on what
the term means. The conceptualization of purpose offered by
Damon, Menon, and Bronk[2] was instrumentally influential in
developing the components of the purpose-centered career education intervention described in this article. Damon and colleagues'
definition shares common ground with others in conceiving of
purpose as a far-reaching goal, or ultimate concern, that people
endow with personal significance, importance, and meaning.[3]
However, for Damon and colleagues, a purpose also needs to be
rooted in beyond-the-self concerns.

NEW DIRECTIONS FOR YOUTH DEVELOPMENT, NO. 132, WINTER 2011 © WILEY PERIODICALS, INC.
Published online in Wiley Online Library (wileyonlinelibrary.com) • DOI: 10.1002/yd.428

59

This additional prosocial dimension may be particularly apt in the career domain, as it dovetails with centuries of thinking about work as a calling. The scholarship on calling often draws from philosophical and theological foundations; notably, Damon and colleagues reached similar conclusions by drawing from the developmental literature.[4] Erikson and Piaget identified the establishment of identities and self-concepts as the critical developmental task in adolescence.[5] Damon, Menon, and Bronk suggested that in confronting this task, adolescents begin to dedicate themselves to abstract beliefs and purposes; that is, they perceive needs beyond themselves and conceive of a purpose that can serve those needs or benefit others.[6] Despite the developmental relevance of purpose, however, little is known about the extent to which it is possible to cultivate a sense of purpose among middle school students using school-based interventions.

Career education programs represent one type of school-based intervention. Such programs are designed to help students establish ideas for using their abilities and interests in their future careers, with a goal of building a satisfying life.[7] Given the importance of work to the establishment of an enduring sense of purpose, the future orientation inherent in adolescent career development, and the embeddedness of early career education programs in many middle schools, such programs may represent an important opportunity to help students explore, identify, and engage a sense of purpose.[8] This article describes Make Your Work Matter, a brief, purpose-centered career education intervention under development, and reports results from a pilot study evaluating its effectiveness.

The goal of cultivating a sense of purpose in career development fits within a broader context of research on the role of purpose in life generally and in work specifically. Purpose bridges present experience to future aspirations and experiences.[9] Research often links purpose with meaning in life and finds that people who believe their lives have meaning and purpose are happier and experience fewer psychological problems than those without a strong sense of meaning and purpose.[10] Those who view their careers as an avenue for expressing purpose tend to be more deeply engaged in their work, more effective team players, more committed to their occupations and organizations, and more satisfied than those without a purpose orientation.[11] Often meaning and purpose at work take the form of a calling—a summons to a particular career in which purpose at work and purpose in life align in the service of a greater good.[12] People with a sense of calling report both career-related and general well-being benefits, including—for those still preparing for their careers—greater career decision self-efficacy, intrinsic work motivation, and meaning in life, as well as greater commitment to their careers, team members at work, and their employer.[13] Thus, melding Damon and colleagues' ideas about purpose with calling theory creates a powerful mix of meaning, purpose, and career aspirations.

Kosine, Steger, and Duncan proposed a purpose-centered, strengths-based approach to career development among adolescents.[14] They proposed five key factors in the cultivation of purpose in early career development. The first, identity, is present as adolescents clarify their interests and project a sense of self onto their future career. Identity formation is encouraged through opportunities for career and personal exploration, through such points of intervention as interpretation of vocational interest inventories and small group discussions that explore topics related to goals and aspirations. The second, self-efficacy, refers to a person's belief that she or he can effectively complete a particular task.[15] Self-efficacy often is studied within specific life domains. Career decision self-efficacy, for example, refers to the belief that one can effectively navigate the career decision process by gathering needed information about the self and the world of work for use in making informed choices. It is associated with vocational identity, career decidedness, hope, goal stability, and positive affect.[16] Kosine and colleagues suggest that self-efficacy can be increased by helping students identify academic and work-related strengths and potential career paths that would capitalize on those strengths. The third factor, metacognition, refers to self-awareness of one's own thought processes.[17] Metacognition is advantageous in career development and is encouraged by helping students reflect on their cognitive processes and articulate effective strategies for making wise decisions and making those decisions wisely.[18] Fourth, culture, which plays a key role in purpose-centered career development, refers to one's demographic uniqueness (for example, gender, ethnicity, socioeconomic status, disability) and how these factors influence career choices. Kosine and colleagues' approach assumes that such factors help shape which careers students will perceive as providing a sense of purpose and should be targeted by interventions that explore how career choices affect cultural values and vice versa.[19] Finally, service for the greater good and recognition of how one's career contributes to society is a key component of purpose-centered career development. Kosine and colleagues recommend helping students recognize the importance of giving back through their careers.[20]

Development of a purpose-centered career intervention: Make Your Work Matter

Make Your Work Matter is a three-module enhancement to traditional career development activities designed to promote a sense of purpose in the early career development of adolescents. Traditional career development for adolescents consists of self-assessments of interests and skills, exploration of occupational information, and goal-setting activities, tasks that help address four of the five factors in Kosine and colleagues' model: identity, self-efficacy, metacognition, and culture.[21] Make Your Work Matter augments traditional career development activities in that it also targets these four factors but emphasizes the fifth factor: service. The three modules are a parent interview, a values card sort, and the One Village Game.

Parent interview

In this module, students conduct a thirty-minute structured interview of a parent or other trusted adult. The interview is designed to stimulate parent-child conversation and thought about the role of work in the context of life. Ideally this interview provides the base for future conversations, aiding adolescents in exploring such factors as identity, self-efficacy, and an appreciation of their unique cultural heritage. Questions include: "Does your work fit well with your values? Please explain." "In what ways does your work impact other people or the community? How does it make you feel when you think about this?" and "What advice can you give me about my future career?"

Values card sort

This module, adapted from the O*NET's Work Importance Locator (WIL), is an individually administered classroom activity designed to introduce students to the concept of work values and facilitate reflection on core work-related values and their implications for career exploration and choice.[22] Reflecting on values provides additional opportunities for adolescents to explore identity and culture and may also facilitate metacognition about personal preferences and tendencies.

For many adolescents, service may emerge as an important value. Modifications from the original WIL included more accessible language, a simplified administration procedure, and recasting the card sort as a vehicle for reflection rather than as an assessment instrument.

Students are given twenty cards, each with a work-related need statement (e.g., "I could try out my own ideas," "My co-workers would be easy to get along with," "I could give directions and instructions to others"). They engage in a simple sorting task in which they rank their five most important career values. Finally, they participate in a reflection activity requiring them to imagine a career in which their top values are consistently satisfied.

One Village Game

The One Village Game is a board game designed to encourage students' thinking about the social function of occupations. The game, developed to target the idea of service, builds on the

Figure 4.1. Sample images from One Village Game cards

assumption that the full range of honest areas of work is important for a well-functioning village, providing the full range of jobs with meaning and dignity. Students divide into teams and begin the game by using a variety of strategies to select eight cards, each with a woman or man in one of twelve occupations representing the full scope of prestige, educational level, and income level (Figure 4.1 provides examples). Each team presents their eight cards, which comprise the professions in that village, and evaluates how well that combination of workers will serve the village and what core village needs will remain unmet. Teams then participate in a "job fair" in which they can trade and obtain new cards, with the goal of a more balanced village that meets more needs.

The game's purpose is to provide a tangible means of communicating how the common needs of the village are best met by mutual service among the wide range of professions, and to illustrate how every profession plays an important role in ensuring the well-being of the village as a whole.

The pilot study

Theory and research suggest that finding a purpose derives from the processes of identity and cognitive development. For many adolescents, developing a self-concept and the ability to think abstractly about the future might arise readily and be easily put to work in developing a purpose. For many others, however, putting these factors together might pose a significant challenge. Few resources are available that assist young people in engaging with the issue of how they can use their talents, energy, and idealism to serve a greater purpose.

We initiated this engagement process by providing resources to a group of adolescents in an intuitively important context: the career education program in their school. This article reports an initial pilot test of a school-based intervention designed to help adolescents explore, discover, and enact a sense of purpose. Our aims were twofold:

- To evaluate whether students participating in the intervention, relative to a quasi-experimental control group, experience improved career development outcomes and a stronger sense of purpose, both of which we hypothesize to be the case
- To collect qualitative (focus group) evaluative data useful for revising and improving the intervention

Method

Participants

The participants were seventy-six eighth-grade students (63 percent girls), with a mean age of 13.88 years ($SD = .47$). Approximately two-thirds (64.5 percent) self-identified as white/European American; 14.7 percent were Latina/o, 1.3 percent were Asian, and 19 percent were multiracial or other. This approximated the distribution of ethnicity in the school and broader community. Participating students provided informed consent, and implicit parental consent also was obtained according to Institutional Review Board–approved procedures.

Procedure

A quasi-experimental design was implemented in which students were assigned to the intervention or control condition based on their membership in one of four sections of eighth-grade English. Students in all four sections had received traditional career education as seventh graders: group interpretation of interest and self-reported skills inventories, exploration of occupational information, and goal-setting exercises. Those in two class sections (the intervention group, with thirty students) also participated in the Make Your Work Matter modules, whereas those in the other two sections (the control group, with forty-six students) participated in standard English curricula that did not include a career unit. The modules were implemented over the course of one week. All participants completed a preintervention and postintervention questionnaire. Finally, ten students from the intervention group, selected by the school counselor to be roughly representative of the eighth-grade cohort, participated in a thirty-minute follow-up focus group in which a structured group interview was facilitated.

Instruments

Because of classroom time constraints and the purpose of the pilot study as an initial evaluation of the intervention, the decision was made to assess pre- and postintervention attitudes using a wide-bandwidth, low-fidelity measurement approach. Therefore, eighteen single-item scales were used to assess a broad range of career development and purpose-related beliefs with a rating scale ranging from 0 = *absolutely untrue*, to 100 = *absolutely true*. Eleven open-ended questions also were administered; the first two assessed students' learning outcomes (for example, "What were the three most important things you learned about your career this week?"), and the remaining nine assessed what students liked, learned from, and would change regarding each of the three modules in the intervention.

Results

Univariate analysis of covariance, with preintervention scores entered as covariates for postintervention scores, was used to examine the intervention effects. Because of the nature of the study as a pilot evaluation of an intervention under development, paired with a sample size that placed a low ceiling on statistical power, we opted to err in the direction of minimizing Type II errors by using a p-value cutoff of .10 without controlling for family-wise error. Results suggested that relative to the control group, the group participating in the Make Your Work Matter intervention reported a clearer sense of direction in their careers ($F = 3.28$, $p = .07$, partial $\eta^2 = .04$), a greater understanding of their interests ($F = 5.77$, $p = .02$, partial $\eta^2 = .07$) and strengths and weaknesses ($F = 7.54$, $p = .01$, partial $\eta^2 = .09$), and felt more prepared for the future ($F = 12.67$, $p = .001$, partial $\eta^2 = .15$). Curiously, they also reported a stronger desire for wealth in their future careers ($F = 3.18$, $p = .08$, partial $\eta^2 = .04$).

No other substantive differences were found between groups, including on items that directly pertain to a sense of purpose, calling, or prosocial attitudes. An analysis of responses to the open-ended questions revealed that most students appeared to understand the purpose of the modules; many expressed career goals incorporating meaningfulness, purpose, calling, and prosocial attitudes and behaviors; and most students expressed that they enjoyed the intervention.

Evaluative data from the focus group were transcribed and analyzed using Johnson, Dunlap, and Benoit's semiquantitative coding strategy for organizing data, which consists of identifying and labeling important themes, then categorizing them based on their relative frequency.[23] Three primary themes emerged in the focus group. First, students tended to exhibit considerable confidence in their current career decision. That is, when asked to describe their career plans, each identified a specific occupation with little hesitation, often even articulating specific universities that could help them pursue their paths. Second, students described enjoying the process of exploring their values through the card sort activity and said that it helped clarify their wants and needs in a career. One student's comment was representative: "It helped me decide what I liked." Although feedback was positive for the parent interview and the One Village Game (for example, "Yeah, that was kind of fun. Our village was perfect."), students found the card sort particularly helpful and indicated that exploring their values and clarifying their strengths and weaknesses was a highly valued outcome. The third theme was that although students indicated that they had already spent time (prior to the intervention) thinking about potential career paths, the intervention helped bring more specific career trajectories into focus, while also yielding information useful for greater self-understanding. One student illustrated this theme: "I knew the jobs I wanted to do, but I guess I just learned more about myself" from participation in the intervention.

Discussion

Although cultivating a sense of purpose is developmentally salient and desirable for adolescents, no interventions (of which we are aware) prior to Make Your Work Matter have been developed and tested that seek to help facilitate a sense of purpose. Results of the pilot study indicated that students participating in a purpose-centered intervention embedded in a career education curriculum, relative to a comparison group that participated in traditional career education only, experienced meaningful improvement in career development attitudes. Specifically, they reported a clearer sense of direction, a better understanding of their interests and strengths and weaknesses, and a greater level of preparedness for the future. These variables are related to Kosine and colleagues' factors of identity, self-efficacy, and (to a lesser extent) metacognition and culture.[24] Participants also reported a stronger desire for wealth, counter to our expectations. This result may reflect a deeper level of achievement motivation than was present among students who participated in traditional career development only; alternatively, the emphasis on finances and economic desires may have been a natural result of reflecting on one's future career in contrast to the control group, which engaged in an English curriculum between pre- and postintervention assessments. A third option is that students' desire for wealth may reflect a prosocially oriented value for philanthropy. Of course, it is possible that aspects of the intervention may have had an opposite effect of what was intended in this regard. The study unfortunately did not assess these four possibilities; further evaluation of the intervention, should this result replicate, should do so.

Surprisingly, no differences were found between the groups on items pertaining more directly to a sense of purpose, calling, or prosocial attitudes. There are several reasons that this might be the case. Methodologically, it is possible that our coarse measures of these outcomes and small sample size failed to provide a level of power sensitive enough to detect differences, despite our efforts to minimize Type II errors. It also is possible that a sense of purpose develops more gradually than would be detected with a postintervention survey administered immediately after the intervention. By not following participants over time, the study cannot assess the possibility that the intervention may help lay a foundation for a sense of purpose that emerges further down the causal chain. Of course, the interventions may not have addressed purpose-catalyzing factors at a sufficient level of depth. However, these null results should be considered in light of students' answers to the open-ended questions, which revealed that students understood what the intervention modules were intended to convey and expressed goals that incorporated meaningfulness, purpose, calling, and prosocial attitudes. Students also expressed enjoyment of the intervention.

Participants in the focus group provided another layer of insight regarding the strengths and weaknesses of the intervention. The result that students had identified specific careers and expressed confidence in their plans to pursue those careers indicates that the intervention may have helped solidify and reinforce their career choice aspirations. This is a favorable outcome, but it must be weighed against research indicating that vocational interests fluctuate in early adolescence, suggesting that aspirations are best held tentatively by students as they engage in a continual process of exploring the range of occupational opportunities.[25] Students also expressed that the values card sort in particular was engaging and useful and that the intervention as a whole provided information that contributed to their self-understanding.

Limitations

The pilot study suffered from limitations typical of any small-scale effort to provide an initial evaluation of a new intervention: a small sample size providing low statistical power, a measurement strategy assessing a broad array of attitudes but without considerable depth or psychometric support, and the use of a quasi-experimental design rather than a true experiment. Because of these factors, results from this study should be considered tentative.

Implications for practice

The results provide useful practical information. For example, based on these results, we are modifying Make Your Work Matter in several ways. First, the parent interview is being revised to encourage a deeper and more thorough level of integration with the rest of the curriculum. Parental involvement has been shown to play an important role in early career development, and we encourage taking deliberate steps to encourage and facilitate such involvement.[26] Second, clearer instructions are being developed to improve the administration of the values card sort activity. As the focus group revealed, this activity was particularly beneficial for students in terms of exploring and clarifying their work values. We urge educators to engage their students in such exploration, with the caveat that work values card sorts are best used as an exploration tool with adolescents rather than as a formal assessment of work values, given their limited work experience. Third, more streamlined rules and clearer objectives are being developed and tested for the One Village Game. Finally, in-class writing assignments are being implemented to facilitate a deeper and more structured and coherent integration and application of thematic lessons learned across the intervention's three modules. Writing is useful in drawing themes and providing coherence to the experience, and furthermore provides a visual reminder of the lessons learned as articulated in the students' own words. The results from this study are useful in developing enhancements to the curriculum, but also highlight specific strategies educators can implement to encourage the purpose-centered career development of their students.

To summarize, practitioners should consider the following strategies:

- Give young people structured ways of getting their parents involved in discussions about career expectations and the idea of meaningful and purposeful work.
- Help young people explore their work values, as we did with our values card sort.
- Look for opportunities to engage young people in conversations about the dignity and interconnectedness of all honest occupations.

Implications for research

The pilot study also lays the groundwork for a large-scale, multischool trial of the improved intervention, using psychometrically supported measurement instruments, that tracks participants longitudinally to provide an appraisal of the longer-term effects of the intervention. Research also can examine each component of the intervention, along with other intervention strategies, using a translational research approach.[27] The result that the intervention improved career development criterion variables more so than criterion variables more directly related to a sense of purpose raises the question of how these sets of outcomes are related. Kosine and colleagues framed vocational identity, self-efficacy, metacognition, and culture as key components of a sense of purpose in career.[28] Their fifth factor, service, is most directly related to typical means of conceptualizing purpose. Basic research is needed that investigates how these factors develop, relate to each other, and work in concert to promote a sense of purpose. Results from such research would serve to inform this and other intervention strategies.

Notes

1. Damon, W. (2008). *The path to purpose: Helping our children find their calling in life.* New York, NY: Free Press.
2. Damon, W., Menon, J., & Bronk, K. C. (2003). The development of purpose during adolescence. *Applied Developmental Science, 7*(3), 119–128.
3. See also McKnight, P. E., & Kashdan, T. B. (2009). Purpose in life as a system that creates and sustains health and well-being: An integrative, testable theory. *Review of General Psychology, 13*(3), 242–251; Reker, G. T., Peacock, E. J., & Wong, P.T.P. (1987). Meaning and purpose in life and well-being: A life span perspective. *Journal of Gerontology, 42*(1), 44–49; Steger, M. F., Frazier, P., Oishi, S., & Kaler, M. (2006). The Meaning in Life Questionnaire: Assessing the presence of and search for meaning in life. *Journal of Counseling Psychology, 53*(1), 80–93.
4. Damon et al. (2003).
5. Erikson, E. H. (1968). *Identity: Youth and crisis.* New York, NY: Norton; Piaget, J. (1990). *The child's conception of the world.* New York, NY: Littlefield Adams.
6. Damon et al. (2003).
7. Turner, S. L., & Lapan, R. T. (2005). Promoting career development and aspirations in school-age youth. In S. Brown & R. Lent (Eds.), *Career development and counseling: Putting theory and research to work* (pp. 417–440). Hoboken, NJ: Wiley.
8. Ryff, C. D., & Singer, B. (1998). The contours of positive human health. *Psychological Inquiry, 9*(1), 1–28; for example, Savickas, M. L. (2003). Career construction: A developmental theory of vocational behavior. In D. Brown & Associates (Eds.), *Career choice and development* (4th ed., pp. 149–205). San Francisco, CA: Jossey-Bass.
9. Kosine, N., Steger, M. F., & Duncan, S. (2008). Purpose-centered career development: A comprehensive model. *Professional School Counseling, 12*(2), 133–136.
10. Steger et al. (2006).
11. Steger, M. F., & Dik, B. J. (2010). Work as meaning. In P. A. Linley, S. Harrington, & N. Page (Eds.), *Oxford handbook of positive psychology and work* (pp. 131–142). New York, NY: Oxford University Press.
12. Dik, B. J., & Duffy, R. D. (2009). Calling and vocation at work: Definitions and prospects for research and practice. *Counseling Psychologist, 37*(3), 424–450.
13. Dik, B. J., Sargent, A. M., & Steger, M. F. (2008). Career development strivings: Assessing goals and motivation in career decision-making and planning. *Journal of Career Development, 35*(1), 23–41; Steger, M. F., Dik, B. J., & Duffy, R. D. (in press). Measuring meaningful work: The Work and Meaning Inventory (WAMI). *Journal of Career Assessment;* Wrzesniewski, A., McCauley, C., Rozin, P., & Schwartz, B. (1997). Jobs, careers, and callings: People's relations to their work. *Journal of Research in Personality, 31*(1), 21–33.
14. Kosine et al. (2008).
15. Bandura, A. (1982). Self-efficacy mechanism in human agency. *American Psychologist, 37*(2), 122–147; Lent, R. W. (2005). A social cognitive view of

career development and counseling. In S. Brown & R. Lent (Eds.), *Career development and counseling: Putting theory and research to work* (pp. 101–127). Hoboken, NJ: Wiley.

16. Betz, N. E., Hammond, M. S., & Multon, K. D. (2005). Reliability and validity of five-level response continua for the Career Decision Self-Efficacy Scale. *Journal of Career Assessment, 13*(2), 131–149.

17. Kosine et al. (2008).

18. Batha, K., & Carroll, M. (2007). Metacognitive training aids decision-making. *Australian Journal of Psychology, 59*(2), 64–69; Symes, B. A., & Stewart, J. B. (1999). The relationship between metacognition and vocational indecision. *Canadian Journal of Counseling, 33*(3), 195–211; Savickas, M. L. (2005). The theory and practice of career construction. In S. Brown & R. Lent (Eds.), *Career development and counseling: Putting theory and research to work* (pp. 42–70). Hoboken, NJ: Wiley.

19. Kosine et al. (2008).

20. Kosine et al. (2008).

21. Kosine et al. (2008).

22. U.S. Department of Labor. (2000). *Work Importance Locator: User's guide.* Washington, DC: Employment and Training Administration.

23. Johnson, B. D., Dunlap, E., & Benoit, E. (2010). Organizing "mountains of words" for data analysis, both qualitative and quantitative. *Substance Use and Misuse, 45*(5), 648–670.

24. Kosine et al. (2008).

25. Low, D.K.S., Yoon, M., Roberts, B. W., & Rounds. J. (2005). The stability of interests from early adolescence to middle adulthood: A quantitative review of longitudinal studies. *Psychological Bulletin, 131*(5), 713–737.

26. Whiston, S. C., & Keller, B. K. (2011). The influences of the family of origin on career development: A review and analysis. *Counseling Psychologist, 32*, 493–568.

27. Tashiro, T., & Mortensen, L. (2006). Translational research: How social psychology can improve psychotherapy. *American Psychologist, 61*(9), 959–966.

28. Kosine et al. (2008).

BRYAN J. DIK *is associate professor of counseling psychology at Colorado State University.*

MICHAEL F. STEGER *is associate professor of counseling psychology and applied social psychology, and director of the Laboratory for the Study of Meaning and Quality of Life, at Colorado State University. He is also affiliated with North-West University in South Africa.*

AMANDA GIBSON *is a 2011 graduate in psychology from Colorado State University.*

WILLIAM PEISNER *is a school counselor at Wellington Middle School in Wellington, Colorado.*

This chapter examines the effects of an intervention promoting the role of purpose and internal control as mechanisms of change for positive youth development and academic achievement in low-socioeconomic-status adolescents.

5

Purpose plus: Supporting youth purpose, control, and academic achievement

Jane Elizabeth Pizzolato,
Elizabeth Levine Brown, Mary Allison Kanny

THE ACHIEVEMENT GAP persists between students of more and less privilege, where privilege includes both racial and economic privilege.[1] Research has shown that on average, students of color and students from low-income communities achieve at lower rates than their higher-income and white peers.[2] Although the achievement gap decreased during the 1970s and 1980s, it began to widen again in the 1990s.[3]

In attempting to understand why this achievement gap persists, two models are most prevalent within the literature. In the first, the achievement gap is explained by discussing deficits in the educational experiences of students from low-income and minority communities. Such discussion tends to focus on human and financial resources, which low-income-serving schools typically lack;

NEW DIRECTIONS FOR YOUTH DEVELOPMENT, NO. 132, WINTER 2011 © WILEY PERIODICALS, INC.
Published online in Wiley Online Library (wileyonlinelibrary.com) • DOI: 10.1002/yd.429

low levels of family involvement regarding both school readiness and school engagement; or negative peer cultures—or some combination of these.[4] An alternative model focuses on student characteristics that may lead to the persistence of the achievement gap. Often the fundamental student characteristic that undergirds all others is motivation to achieve. Research on the relationship between aspirations and achievement has consistently identified motivation as the strongest predictor of achievement.[5] Students who are motivated aspire to future academic success and show signs of purpose, which leads to achievement. However, Cokley demonstrated that even when students of color exhibit high levels of intrinsic motivation to succeed, their achievement remains depressed compared to that of their white peers.[6] Thus, it seems there are additional, or possibly alternative, variables that should be considered when working with youth from low-income and minority communities to improve their academic achievement.

Internal control over academic success

Although motivation may indicate desire to achieve, one missing piece of the motivation-achievement process is how students move from wanting to achieve to actually achieving. Control theory asserts that the more people believe they are in control of their own achievement, the greater the likelihood is that they will achieve.[7] As Connell noted, knowing who or what is in control and ultimately believing yourself to be in control is strongly related to achievement.[8] With a colleague, Connell developed this argument by laying out how greater control leads to greater feelings of competency, which then contribute to greater levels of achievement.[9] Skinner, Zimmer-Gembeck, and Connell later expanded on this idea by showing that greater perceptions of control are related not just to greater competence but to more positive perceptions of teachers and school as well.[10]

It seems, then, that perceptions of control are important to how students think about not only their academic abilities but also their abilities to be successful within their school context. In other words, more than believing that they possess certain academic abilities, strong perceptions of control may also be useful in helping students think that they have the ability to become what they hope to be, even in the face of challenges.[11]

Youth purpose

Perceptions of control speak to the degree to which students see themselves as in charge of their academic achievement. More broadly, however, it seems important to examine youth's ability to envision themselves as successful adults and connect those future images to current school behavior.[12]

Recent findings suggest that personal goals are associated with academic achievement for adolescents, particularly for adolescents from less privileged communities.[13] Among the personal goals that adolescents set, Nurmi noted that they identify personal aspirations or future orientations related to occupational goals the most.[14] Identifying career paths and how to navigate trajectories to achieve those career aspirations is an active part of identity development for adolescents; however, new literature indicates that adolescents need to know their career goal and how to achieve it, as well as to develop a sense of meaning and purpose regarding their identified future occupational aspiration.[15] When defining a purpose about what these adolescents want to achieve in their lives, Yeager and Bundick stated that "young people seek to understand not only how their work goals incorporate who they want to be but also how their work will allow them to make a contribution and feel like they have a purpose."[16] In short, the role of purpose seems to contribute to how adolescents perceive themselves in the future, and it also serves as a psychosocial influence on achievement.

Although studies have assessed adolescents' purpose as the ability to manage and adapt to challenging situations, positive-psychology researchers over the past decade defined *purpose* as a means to understanding positive youth development.[17] In accordance with positive psychology, we operationally define *purpose* here as "a stable and generalized intention to accomplish something that is at once meaningful to the self and of consequence to the world beyond the self."[18] Notably, purpose encompasses establishing long-term goals that foster meaning in adolescents' lives, viewing long-term goals as future accomplishments, and understanding how long-term goals contribute beyond self to our world broadly. Thus, the concept of purpose moves beyond goal-oriented aspirations, which are typically suggested in motivation research but have not been shown to close the aspiration-achievement gap.

Primarily studies on purpose coincide with inquiries into emotional, social, cognitive, religious, and moral development.[19] In fact, previous reviews on purpose indicated that purpose evolved initially from testing measures on purpose.[20] However, these studies explore purpose using varying definitions of the term and neglect to address the developmental modifications necessary to test purpose in youth. Although initial studies on purpose struggled to understand its role in understanding positive youth development, some recent inquiries show that purpose influences adolescents' future orientation, academic achievement, and coping strategies.[21] Moreover, recent qualitative studies by the Stanford Youth Purpose Project indicate that highly purposeful adolescents are the exception in classrooms nationally, with only 20 percent of a diverse national sample demonstrating clear purpose toward their academic work.[22]

Despite recent inquiries into the important role of purpose on positive youth development and academic achievement broadly, we still understand little regarding the role of purpose in helping adolescents aspire to future goals and achieve academically. As Reilly discussed, there are several developmentally appropriate interventions needed to assess adolescents', and particularly less privileged adolescents', conceptualizations of purpose over time and how such purpose relates to specific life domains (for example, family and academics).[23] Given our interest here in understanding the achievement of students from a low-performing school in a low-income community, assessing adolescents' purpose at the academic or school level seems to be both appropriate and an area of study that lacks review.

Intervention

Based on research, an intervention program aimed to enhance perceptions of control and youth purpose was proposed. The intervention consisted of bimonthly small group sessions in a semiprivate environment at the high school. The intervention program lasted eighteen weeks during the 2007–2008 academic year. The structure and format of the intervention sessions were modeled after Oyserman and colleagues' intervention work with African American students to develop plans and skills for achieving their aspirations, as well as skills for coping with threats to their achievement (for example, unsupportive or ridiculing peers).[24]

In terms of the intervention sessions themselves, postsecondary purpose was identified first. Following this, participants engaged in discussions regarding how to use, enact, and achieve their purpose. The third and fourth sessions focused on identifying and evaluating purpose through activities of building a time line for achieving mini-goals and identifying social networks supportive of these goals and values. Next, sessions 5 through 7 introduced discussions and activities designed to develop participants' perceptions of control.

Purpose

The purpose of this study was twofold as it relates to the following research questions: (1) Was the intervention effective in developing internal control over academic success and purpose? (2) If adolescents improve their internal control over academic success and their purpose in life, how do these developments help explain achievement, as measured by grade point average (GPA), after controlling for previous academic achievement?

Method

This study evaluated the effectiveness of an intervention designed to promote purpose development and internal control over academic success in high school students from a low-socioeconomic-status community. We were particularly interested in whether and how the inclusion of purpose development helped explain academic achievement.

This study was conducted in a low-income community pseudonymously named Milltown in western Pennsylvania. The median per capita income is $14,608; based on 2000 U.S. Census data, approximately one-third of the children under age eighteen were living below the poverty line. The one high school in the town serves 269 students in grades 9 through 12. The student body is racially split, with 170 students identifying as black or African American and 99 students self-identifying as white. Of these students, 223 were eligible for free lunch and 43 for reduced-price lunch, leaving only 3 in the high school who were not eligible.

Participants

The 209 participants were recruited from the high school during spring 2007 when the study was advertised in English classes. Following receipt of both parental consent and student assent, an intervention group of 30 was selected based on analyses of internal control over academic success and purpose in life measured at the time of consent and assent. We aimed to include students who fell one to two standard deviations below the mean on both measures, because such scores indicated need and room for growth. Although a power analysis indicated that 28 participants were needed for an intervention group, 30 were originally included in anticipation of potential dropouts. A matched peer group was designed based on the demographic variables (such as sex and race), internal control,

Table 5.1. Group frequencies and means

	Intervention group	Matched group
Females	23	23
Males	7	7
African American or black	23	23
White	6	6
Mixed race	1	1
Mean internal control at time 1 (SD)	3.08 (.61)	3.19 (.67)
Mean purpose at time 1 (SD)	90.21 (10.77)	87.9 (17.33)
Mean internal control change score* (SD)	.45 (.60)	−.03[a] (.50)
Mean purpose change score** (SD)	79.94 (31.33)	36.97 (26.42)
Mean GPA at time 1 (SD)	2.58 (.73)	2.57 (.70)
Mean GPA at time 2 (SD)	2.71 (.63)	2.66 (.71)

[a]Mean internal control over academic achievement decreased by .03 between time points 1 and 2.
$*t = 3.38, p < .001. **t = 5.74, p < .0001.$

and purpose scores at preassessment. The demographics of the sample and matched peer groups are provided in Table 5.1.

Data collection procedures

Data were collected from all participants twice, in September 2007 and May 2008, to coincide with the start and end of the academic year. Surveys were used to assess internal control over academic success and purpose in life. Specifically, Connell's (1985) Multidimensional Measure of Children's Perception of Control was administered to gauge internal control. There are nine subscales within this instrument; however, given the focus of this study we used the 37-item subscale regarding the degree to which participants believed they could control their attributions for success and failure in the classroom.[25] The revised Purpose in Life Test (PIL-R), an eighteen-item survey that asks students to respond to statement stems on a seven-point Likert type scale, was used to measure purpose in life.[26] Because we were working with a youth population and could not guarantee confidentiality if the students reported suicidal ideation, we deleted the two questions that addressed this issue. We also collected students' grade reports at

NEW DIRECTIONS FOR YOUTH DEVELOPMENT • DOI: 10.1002/yd

the end of the school year so we had a record of their GPA across time. Prior achievement was operationalized here as the students' cumulative GPA at the end of the previous academic year, and their ending academic achievement was operationalized as their cumulative GPA at the end of the 2007–2008 academic year.

Data analysis procedures

Prior to data analyses being run for the specific research questions, change scores were computed for both internal control over academic success and purpose in life. Table 5.1 provides the mean change scores for both the intervention and control groups, in addition to mean GPA at both time points. Once these scores were computed, an independent samples *t*-test and hierarchical multiple regression were run to investigate the research questions. The specifics of these analyses and the results are discussed in the following section.

Results

Was the intervention effective?

Independent samples *t*-tests found significant differences between the internal control over academic success and purpose-in-life change scores of students participating in the intervention and those not participating in the intervention. With respect to internal control over academic achievement, the mean change for students participating in the intervention was significantly larger than for students not participating ($t = 3.38$, $p < .001$). The *t*-test of differences in mean purpose change scores showed a similar pattern at a greater magnitude ($t = 5.74$, $p < .0001$). These large, significant differences suggest that the intervention was effective in promoting change in the areas of internal control and purpose.

How do attributions and purpose contribute to achievement?

A hierarchical multiple regression was run to examine whether and how much change in internal control over academic success and

purpose in life contributed to explaining variance in students' ending GPAs after controlling for their prior achievement. Students'
entering GPAs were entered in step 1. Step 2 included change
scores on both internal attributions and purpose in life. The model
was significant ($F(60) = 613.19$, $p < .001$) and explained 91.1 percent of the variance in students' ending GPAs. The majority of the
variance was accounted for by students' entering GPAs ($r^2 = .71$);
however, adding in the change scores in internal control over academic achievement and purpose in life offered a further explanation of 20.1 percent of the variance.

Discussion

This study built on existing research that independently investi-
gated how control and purpose in life might contribute to youth
achievement. By bringing both pieces in an intervention study
together, our findings speak to two issues: the possibility of
increasing purpose in life and the potential achievement benefits of
combining purpose with an academic attitude like internal control
beliefs.

Our findings demonstrated that it was possible to increase students' sense of purpose through a short-term intervention.
Although both groups of students showed gains in purpose in life,
the gains that students made in the intervention were markedly
higher. Given that changes in purpose and internal control were
able to explain 20.1 percent of participants' ending GPAs, it seems
that purpose may be a potential area of interest for K-12 practitioners working with students who are academically achieving below
average. Academic intervention programs aimed toward developing students' sense of purpose and internal control might offer a
complementary, if not alternative, approach to remediation in
schools serving academically at-risk youth who demonstrate low
sense of purpose.

When adding control into the mix of variables, it is worth
noting that although the matched group had a slightly higher

perception of internal control over academic achievement when beginning the academic year, on average they actually decreased in their perception of internal control over the course of the year. Although this was not a large decrease, the fact that these students tended to maintain or decrease their perceptions of internal control over the year, while their peers in the intervention group increased their perceptions of internal control, implies that the intervention was not only promoting perceptions of internal control but also buffering students against whatever force was causing the matched group to decrease their perceptions of internal control over academic achievement. In addition, it seems that addressing purpose and internal control within the same intervention may have helped students develop or commit to their purpose, and this may have spurred more thoughtful consideration of how they could achieve their purpose. Such a motivational process, coupled with the explicit work they were doing on internal control as part of the intervention, might have helped students feel simultaneously more internally in control and more committed to their purpose.

In relationship to the literature on youth purpose, our findings suggest that purpose plus internal control are positive contributors to academic achievement and that both can be developed through purposeful programming. Research has shown that purpose consists of a sense of meaning regarding identified future aspirations and that this purpose emerges from a combination of a personal desire to be something or someone in particular and a desire to contribute to the broader society.[27] For high school students, achievement in school is often a prerequisite to achieving their purpose. For example, if a student sees legal advocacy as part of her or his purpose, postsecondary education will likely be a requirement for achieving this goal, and entrance into postsecondary education depends on high school graduation. In short, academic achievement serves as a gatekeeper to purpose achievement for many youth, particularly those who are attending low-performing schools where they may have few resources to support their success when compared to their more privileged peers. The findings of our study suggest, however, that achievement may be well served by considering both purpose and internal control. The inclusion of internal control helps clarify for students that they are important predictors of and mechanisms for achieving their own purpose.

Conclusion

Research in issues of youth purpose and internal control has offered myriad explanations for understanding the ways youth conceive and make sense of motivation in relation to academic achievement. What has remained unclear, however, is the potential linkages that exist between these theories as a means for creating pathways for academic success. The fundamental gap between a student's level of motivation and academic achievement is addressed in this study by an examination of the paired effect of students' internal control of academic achievement and perceptions of sense of purpose. This study extends our current understandings of the ways youth may move conceptually from the desire to achieve academically to the realization of such aspirations through positive development. The coupled effect of a sense of internal control and purpose as fostered through an intervention program had significant effects on the academic achievement of high school students. As such, it seems that students may require a certain degree of competency in both their perceptions of internal control and youth purpose in order to navigate the paths toward their aspirations successfully.

Targeted interventions focusing on both purpose and internal control may serve as a potential means to fostering academic achievement among youth in high-risk academic environments. The individualized, small-group nature of this intervention allowed participants to operationalize concepts within their lives, identifying tangible goals and identifying strategies for achieving them. Inherent in such conversations was honest acknowledgment of the obstacles or barriers to achievement and subsequent development of constructive means for overcoming them. These types of intervention dialogues could potentially take place in multiple venues with a variety of individuals with whom students interact, such as teachers, counselors, and parents. As such, the practical implications of this study suggest that such interventions that encourage youth purpose and internal control may potentially be implemented in various ways.

The practical and theoretical implications of this study are underscored by the notion that the academic achievement of youth might be addressed through avenues related to psychological development of purpose and control. Future research on this topic ought to address the specific ways in which intervention programs can most effectively develop internal control, in conjunction with a sense of purpose among youth so as to encourage higher levels of academic achievement.

Notes

1. NCES. (2010). *Achievement gaps: How Hispanic and White students in public schools perform in mathematics and reading on the National Assessment of Educational Progress* (NCES 2011–459). Washington, DC: Hemphill, F. C., and Vanneman, A.

2. Brantlinger, E. (1992). Unmentionable futures: Postschool planning for low-income teenagers. *School Counselor, 39*(4), 281–291; Chapa, J., & Valencia, R. R. (1993). Latino population growth, demographic characteristics, and educational stagnation: An examination of recent trends. *Hispanic Journal of Behavioral Sciences, 15*(2), 165–187; Hedges, L. V., & Nowell, A. (1999). Changes in the black-white achievement test scores. *Sociology of Education, 72*(2), 111–135; O'Connor, C., Hill, L. D., & Robinson, S. R. (2009). Who's at risk in school and what's race got to do with it? *Review of Research in Education, 33*(1), 1–34. doi:10.3102/0091732X08327991; Wilson, T., Karimpour, R., & Rodkin, P. C. (2011). African American and European American students' peer groups during early adolescence: Structure, status, and academic achievement. *Journal of Early Adolescence, 31*(1), 74–98.

3. Lee, J. (2002). Racial and ethnic achievement gap trends: Reversing the progress toward equity? *Educational Researcher, 31*(1), 3–12. doi:10.3102/0013189X031001003.

4. Bourdieu, P. (1997). The forms of capital. In A. H. Halsey, H. Lauder, P. Brown, & A. S. Wells (Eds.), *Education: Culture, economy, and society* (pp. 40–58). New York: Oxford University Press; Payne, R. K. (2001). *A framework for understanding poverty*. Highlands, TX: aha! Process; Song, S. Y., & Pyon, S. M. (2008). Cultural deficit model. In N. J. Salkind (Ed.), *Encyclopedia of educational psychology* (Vol. 2, pp. 216–217). Thousand Oaks, CA: Sage; Trueba,

E.H.T. (1988). Culturally based explanations of minority students' academic achievement. *Anthropology and Education Quarterly, 19*(3), 270–287.

5. Ames, C. (1992). Classrooms: Goals, structures, and student motivation. *Journal of Educational Psychology, 84*(3), 261–271; Eccles, J. S., Wigfield, A., & Schiefele, U. (1998). Motivation to succeed. In W. Damon (Series Ed.) & N. Eisenberg (Vol. Ed.), *Handbook of child psychology: Vol. 3. Social, emotional, and personality development* (5th ed., pp. 1017–1095). Hoboken, NJ: Wiley; Joselowsky, F. (2007). Youth engagement, high school reform, and improved learning outcomes: Building systemic approaches for youth engagement. *NASSP Bulletin, 91*(3), 257–276.

6. Cokley, K. O. (2003). What do we know about the motivation of African American students? Challenging the "anti-intellectual" myth. *Harvard Educational Review, 73*(4), 524–558.

7. Eccles, J. S., & Wigfield, A. (2002). Motivational beliefs, values, and goals. *Annual Review of Psychology, 53*, 109–132.

8. Connell, J. P. (1985). A new multidimensional measure of children's perceptions of control. *Child Development, 56*(4), 1018–1041.

9. Connell, J. P. (2003). *Getting off the dime: First steps toward implementing First Things First.* Report prepared for the U.S. Department of Education. Philadelphia, PA: Institute for Research and Reform in Education; Connell, J. P., & Wellborn, J. G. (1991). Competence, autonomy and relatedness: A motivational analysis of self-system processes. In M. Gunnar & L. A. Sroufe (Eds.), *Minnesota Symposium on Child Psychology* (Vol. 23). Chicago, IL: University of Chicago Press.

10. Skinner, E. A., Zimmer-Gembeck, M. J., & Connell, J. P. (1998). Individual differences and the development of perceived control. *Monographs of the Society for Research in Child Development, 63*(2–3), 1–220.

11. Wentzel, K., & Wigfield, A. (2007). Motivation interventions that work: Themes and remaining issues. *Educational Psychologist, 42*(4), 261–271.

12. Oyserman, D., Terry, K., & Bybee, D. (2002). A possible selves intervention to enhance school involvement. *Journal of Adolescence, 24*, 313–326.

13. Massey, E. K., Gebhardt, W. A., & Garnefski, N. (2008). Adolescent goal content and pursuit: A review of the literature from the past 16 years. *Developmental Review, 28*, 421–460; Oyserman, D., Bybee, D., & Terry, K. (2006). Possible selves and academic outcomes: How and when possible selves impel action. *Journal of Personality and Social Psychology, 91*(1), 188–204.

14. Nurmi, J. (1991). How do adolescents see their future? A review of the development of future orientation and planning. *Developmental Review, 11*, 1–59.

15. Csikszentmihalyi, M., & Schneider, B. (2000). *Becoming adult: How teenagers prepare for the world of work.* New York, NY: Basic Books; Eccles, J. S., & Wigfield, A. (2002). Motivational beliefs, values, and goals. *Annual Review of Psychology, 53*, 109–132; Erikson, E. (1968). *Identity: Youth and crisis.* New York, NY: Norton; Yeager, D. S., & Bundick, M. J. (2009). The role of purposeful work goals in promoting meaning in life and in schoolwork during adolescence. *Journal of Adolescent Research, 24*(4), 423–452.

16. Yeager & Bundick. (2009). P. 426.

17. Damon, W., Menon, J., & Bronk, K. C. (2003). The development of purpose during adolescence. *Applied Developmental Science*, 7(3), 119–128.

18. Damon et al. (2003). P. 121.

19. Damon et al. (2003).

20. Chickering, A. W., & Reisser, L. (1993). *Education and identity* (2nd ed.). San Francisco, CA: Jossey-Bass; Crumbaugh, J. C., & Maholick, L. T. (1969). *Manual of instructions for the Purpose in Life Test*. Munster, IN: Psychometric Affiliates; Francis, L. J. (2000). The relationship between Bible reading and purpose in life among 13–15 year-olds. *Mental Health, Religion and Culture*, 3, 27–36; Winston, R. B., Miller, T. K., & Cooper, D. L. (1999). *Student developmental task and lifestyle assessment*. Athens, GA: Student Development.

21. Damon, W. (2008b). *The path to purpose*. New York, NY: Free Press; Fry, P. S. (1998). The development of personal meaning and wisdom in adolescence: A reexamination of moderating and consolidating factors and influences. In P.T.P. Wong & P. S. Fry (Eds.), *The human quest for meaning: A handbook of psychological research and clinical applications* (pp. 91–110). Mahwah, NJ: Erlbaum; Mariano, J. M., & Savage, J. (2009). Exploring the language of youth purpose: References to positive states and coping styles by adolescents with different kinds of purpose. *Journal of Research in Character Education*, 7(1), 1–24.

22. Damon, W. (2008a). The moral North Star: How do we help students understand that academic excellence can get them where they want to go? *Educational Leadership*, 66(2), 8–12.

23. Reilly, T. (2010, March). *How can interventions to support purpose or purpose precursors be designed in ways that are age-appropriate?* Paper presented at the Society for Research on Adolescence Biennial Meeting, Philadelphia, PA.

24. Oyserman, D., Gant, L., & Ager, J. (1995). A socially contextualized model of African American identity: Possible selves and school persistence. *Journal of Personality and Social Psychology*, 69(6), 1216–1232.

25. Connell. (1985).

26. Crumbaugh & Maholick. (1969).

27. Yeager & Bundick. (2009).

JANE ELIZABETH PIZZOLATO *is an assistant professor at the University of California, Los Angeles Graduate School of Education and Information Studies.*

ELIZABETH LEVINE BROWN *is an assistant professor at the College of Education and Human Development at George Mason University.*

MARY ALLISON KANNY *is a doctoral student at the University of California, Los Angeles Graduate School of Education and Information Studies.*

Asking young people to reflect on and talk about their purpose in life can have lasting psychological benefits, including increased goal directedness and greater life satisfaction.

6

The benefits of reflecting on and discussing purpose in life in emerging adulthood

Matthew J. Bundick

ONCE THE EXCLUSIVE purview of philosophy and religion, purpose in life has been a topic of burgeoning interest in the field of psychology. However, from the psychological perspective, the question has little to do with what *the* purpose of life is; instead, the focus is more on what each person understands the purpose of his or her own life to be and how this understanding and the pursuit of one's purpose affect and are affected by other psychological and behavioral constructs. Though people may have more than one purpose, for simplicity's sake "purpose" will be used here in the singular form to denote the presence of one or more purposes. Indeed, there have been many recent theoretical and empirical advances in understanding the role of purpose in human thought and behavior.[1]

Purpose in life has been studied at various developmental stages across the life span, from early adolescence through old age,

NEW DIRECTIONS FOR YOUTH DEVELOPMENT, NO. 132, WINTER 2011 © WILEY PERIODICALS, INC.
Published online in Wiley Online Library (wileyonlinelibrary.com) • DOI: 10.1002/yd.430

though recently youth purpose and purpose in college have garnered particular attention.[2] The developmentally adaptive role of purpose has been demonstrated in investigations of youth across the adolescent years.[3] Emerging adulthood, commonly understood to encompass the years between late adolescence and early adulthood (roughly, ages eighteen to twenty-five), typically marked by identity exploration, instability, self-focus, revision of life priorities and goals, and possibilities, represents a singularly important life phase in the development of purpose.[4] Identity development, an integral aspect of establishing a life purpose, is ongoing and formative in these years.[5] What and who one wants to be is particularly salient as young people navigate the normative transition from bearing few significant life commitments and responsibilities in high school or college to the shouldering of many, such as starting a career, getting married, and having children.[6]

Definitional issues

Although conceptualizations of purpose have commonly been rooted in the seminal philosophical writings of Viktor Frankl, scholars have offered varying conceptualizations.[7] Some have focused on the degree to which one sees one's life as coherent and understandable; others attend more to the global sense that one's life is significant.[8] Damon, Menon, and Bronk refer to purpose as "a stable and generalized intention to accomplish something that is at once meaningful to the self and of consequence to the world beyond the self."[9] This definition highlights the far-reaching, abstract life goal aspect of purpose, which has as "its necessary characteristic . . . not its concreteness but the sense of direction that it provides in creating an objective" to be pursued, which in turn organizes one's lower-level goals, decisions, and actions.[10] Furthermore, it suggests a meaningful goal directedness, an orientation toward and pursuit of one's life goals. Similarly, Kashdan and McKnight have suggested that purpose is "a central, self-organizing life aim" that is a predominant component of one's identity, provides a framework for one's goals and actions, and motivates one to allocate personal resources toward its actualization.[11] Notably, Damon and colleagues emphasize that purpose has a necessarily self-transcendent aim that motivates one to commit to and engage in prosocial, generative behaviors in adolescence and beyond.[12]

Relations with psychological health

The psychological research literature has shown links between purpose and a variety of indicators of positive mental health in adolescence through adulthood. Various measures of purpose in life have been found to be significantly correlated with well-being indicators such as personal growth, self-actualization, life satisfaction, and global measures of psychological well-being in populations ranging from college students to older adults.[13] However, the "purpose" measures used in many of these studies often tap only into a general sense of meaning in life and do not specify a life goal component that has come to be accepted as central to contemporary definitions. Some investigations showing relations among purpose and indicators of psychological well-being have focused more explicitly on the goal-directedness component of purpose, while others highlight the degree to which one has identified a purpose for one's life.[14]

Intervention studies

In the subfield of positive psychology, intervention research has recently received much attention and has shown great promise.[15] Areas of intervention that have demonstrated positive results in nonclinical samples include gratitude, happiness, and positive writing.[16] However, research on ways in which purpose might be enhanced has been sparse.[17]

There has been some relevant intervention work involving constructs similar to purpose that provide encouragement. Harrist,

Carlozzi, McGovern, and Harrist have demonstrated in a sample of college students that talking about one's life goals can have short-term benefits for positive mood and physical health.[18] MacLeod, Coates, and Hetherton showed that training focused on goal setting and future planning in a sample of mostly young adults led to increased life satisfaction three weeks later.[19] Although the interventions were relevant to purpose, these studies assessed neither outcomes related to purpose nor whether the effects were lasting.

Present study

To address the gap in the literature regarding purpose interventions (namely, in the emerging adult years that are formative for purpose development), and to further explore relations among purpose and psychological well-being, the study I examine in this article endeavors to test whether deeply reflecting on and discussing one's purpose in life may have lasting effects toward contributing to both later purpose and later life satisfaction. Furthermore, I investigate whether any such benefits for later life satisfaction may be attributable, at least in part, to changes in purpose. The study posits the following hypotheses:

Hypothesis 1a: Deep reflection on and discussion of one's purpose in life lead to benefits for the purpose-identification component of purpose.

Hypothesis 1b: Deep reflection on and discussion of one's purpose in life lead to benefits for the goal-directedness component of purpose.

Hypothesis 1c: Deep reflection on and discussion of one's purpose in life lead to benefits for life satisfaction.

Hypothesis 2a: The benefits of deep reflection on and discussion of one's purpose in life toward life satisfaction are attributable to changes in purpose identification.

NEW DIRECTIONS FOR YOUTH DEVELOPMENT • DOI: 10.1002/yd

Hypothesis 2b: The benefits of deep reflection on and discussion of one's purpose in life toward life satisfaction are attributable to changes in goal-directedness.

Method

The study employed a subsample of a larger study of youth purpose.[20] The study participants were 102 students from two institutions of higher education in northern California (one large state university and one large community college) who completed a survey in March and April 2007 (the pretest) and again in December 2007 (the posttest). Thirty-eight of these participants were randomly selected to participate in a follow-up interview within two weeks of completing the pretest survey. Although the primary purpose of this interview was for data collection for the larger study, it was believed that (and the study presented here investigates whether) engaging in the interview would serve as an intervention toward increasing purpose.

The interview was conducted one-on-one and in person with a trained interviewer, typically in a casual setting such as on a bench on campus or at a local coffee shop and on average lasted approximately forty-five minutes.[21] The interview was designed to induce reflection and deep thought about one's purpose in life, core values, and most important life goals. After the participant shared these goals, the interviewer invited him or her to explore the reasons behind them, discuss ways in which the person is currently pursuing or has future plans to pursue these goals, and consider how these goals are related to other aspects of his or her life. The protocol included probes to ensure that the interviewee was genuinely considering and engaging in deep thought about the questions. Though it may seem surprising that a forty-five-minute one-time interview could have important and lasting effects as hypothesized here, the efficacy of many similar small social-psychological interventions has been demonstrated across a number of studies.[22]

The mean age of these participants at the time of the pretest survey collection was 21.2 years ($SD = 0.5$ years). Participants were 64 percent female and racially/ethnically diverse: Caucasian (39 percent), Asian American (26 percent), Hispanic/Latino (16 percent), Pacific Islander (9 percent), African American (3 percent), and Native American (2 percent). Approximately 4 percent of the sample self-identified as multiethnic.

Measures

Purpose identification

The Meaning in Life Questionnaire—Presence subscale (MLQ-P), a five-item Likert scale, was used to operationalize purpose identification.[23] Although a popular measure of global meaning in life, the item content of the scale is primarily geared toward assessing the degree to which one has identified a purposeful life goal (a sample item is, "I have found a satisfying life purpose"). The MLQ-P has been shown to be psychometrically sound and has demonstrated strong convergent and discriminant validity.[24] Reliabilities at both pretest and posttest were high ($\alpha_{pre} = .90$, $\alpha_{post} = .89$).

Goal directedness

A short version of the Purpose in Life subscale of Ryff's Psychological Well-Being measure was used to operationalize goal directedness.[25] It is a nine-item Likert scale designed to assess the degree to which one "has goals, intentions, and a sense of direction" in life.[26] It has been shown to be psychometrically sound and has demonstrated strong convergent and discriminant validity (a sample item is, "Some people wander aimlessly through life, but I am not one of them"). Reliabilities at both pretest and posttest were high ($\alpha_{pre} = .87$, $\alpha_{post} = .88$).

Life satisfaction

The Satisfaction with Life Scale is a five-item questionnaire designed to measure people's cognitive judgments of their global life satisfaction.[27] Its psychometric properties are well documented, and it has been validated in a wide variety of populations.[28] Reliabilities at both pretest and posttest were high (α_{pre} = .87, α_{post} = .84).

Results

Mean scores for the interview group and the noninterview group on each of the pretest and posttest measures are shown in Table 6.1. Hypotheses 1a, 1b, and 1c predicted that the purpose interview would provide benefits to the interviewees relative to the noninterviewees. To test these hypotheses, t-tests were run on difference scores (posttest scores minus pretest scores) for each of the three outcome variables (see Figure 6.1). For the purpose identification measure, there was no statistical difference between the mean difference scores for the interview group and the noninterview group ($t(100)$ = 0.23, Cohen's d = 0.05, p = 0.41, one-tailed test). For goal directedness, the difference between the group

Table 6.1. Pretest and posttest means and standard deviations for each variable and condition

Variable	Pretest Mean	Posttest Mean
Interview group		
Purpose identification	5.17 (1.30)	4.62 (1.03)
Goal directedness	5.27 (1.13)	5.54 (1.04)
Life satisfaction	4.57 (1.29)	4.69 (1.25)
Noninterview group		
Purpose identification	4.94 (1.33)	4.33 (0.92)
Goal directedness	5.17 (1.09)	5.04 (1.20)
Life satisfaction	4.46 (1.38)	4.23 (1.30)

Note: Standard deviations are in parentheses.

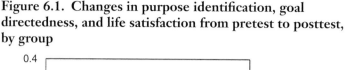

Figure 6.1. Changes in purpose identification, goal directedness, and life satisfaction from pretest to posttest, by group

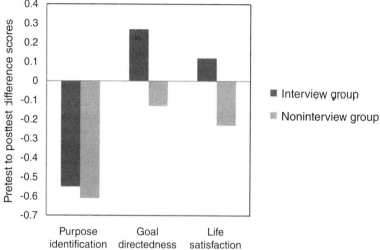

mean difference scores was statistically significant in the hypothesized direction ($t(100) = 2.36$, Cohen's $d = 0.47$, $p \le 0.01$, one-tailed test). For life satisfaction, the difference between the group mean difference scores was also statistically significant in the hypothesized direction ($t(100) = 2.36$, Cohen's $d = 0.36$, $p \le 0.05$, one-tailed test).

Hypotheses 2a and 2b predicted that the benefits of the interview for life satisfaction would be at least in part attributable to changes in purpose identification and goal directedness. That is, lasting benefits in life satisfaction for the interviewees may not have been entirely a direct result of engaging in the interview; instead, they may have been indirect, stemming from the benefits in purpose identification or goal directedness, or both, which are known to be predictive of life satisfaction. This process, known as mediation, can be tested using a series of regression analyses.

Hypothesis 2a could not be tested because the interview did not show benefits for purpose identification (a prerequisite condition for mediation).[29] However, hypothesis 2b could be tested, as there

was evidence that the interview led to benefits for both goal directedness and life satisfaction. Additional regression analyses showed
that change in goal directedness was significantly related to change
in life satisfaction ($\beta = .28$, $p < .01$), which represents the third and
final condition for testing mediation. Hypothesis 2b was tested
using indirect effects analysis, which employs a specialized regression technique known as bootstrapping.[30] This analysis did provide
evidence for mediation ($\beta = .12$, SE $= .08$, 95 percent CI $= [0.01 –
0.33]$), supporting hypothesis 2b. However, this result also suggests
that only some of the effect of engaging in the interview on later
life satisfaction was indirect; thus, the interview likely set other
processes in motion that led to benefits in life satisfaction nine
months later. Although these were not tested in the study, this may
represent an area ripe for future research.

Discussion

The study presented here had two primary goals. First, it investi-
gated whether engaging in a one-time session of reflection on and
discussion about one's purpose in life (in the context of an interview) could lead to benefits for both purpose and life satisfaction
nine months later. Second, it explored whether any benefits of
engaging in such an exercise toward later life satisfaction might be
at least partially attributable to changes in purpose. The findings
provide some, though not uniform, support for the hypotheses.

Regarding hypothesis 1a, there was no support for the contention that deep reflection on and discussion of one's purpose in life
increases the degree to which one believes one has found a purpose
in life nine months later. However, such reflection and discussion
was found to lead on average to benefits for the goal-directedness
component of purpose nine months later (hypothesis 1b). Specifically, the purpose discussion may have buffered against what
appears to be a normative decline in goal directedness in the
emerging adult years. Similarly, the results provide evidence for
the contention that reflection on and discussion of one's purpose

may buffer against an apparent normative decline in life satisfaction over the same time span (hypothesis 1c). This finding builds on previous work showing the benefits of discussing one's life goals, and extends these findings well beyond the short-term benefits previously uncovered.

Since purpose identification was not affected by engaging in reflection on and discussion of one's purpose, hypothesis 2a could not be tested. However, the results do provide some evidence for hypothesis 2b that changes in goal directedness partially mediate the benefits of engaging in reflection on and discussion of one's purpose toward later life satisfaction. At the same time, some of the direct effect of the purpose discussion on life satisfaction remained.

The findings regarding the demonstrated benefits of a one-time intensive session of reflection on and discussion about one's purpose in life on goal directedness many months later might be explained at least in part by the idea that this purpose discussion might act as a triggering event. This triggering event could impel an emerging adult, who is likely in this life stage to be predisposed to identity exploration, to reflect on life beyond the interview and reconsider his or her life path.[31] Graber and Brooks-Gunn suggested that life transitional periods, such as the transition from adolescence to adulthood, are times of "heightened sensitivity" for "transition-linked turning points."[32] This trigger could thus function as an important life turning point.[33] The idea of turning points has been proposed as part of life course theory and narrative identity to refer to episodes that serve as catalysts for long-term behavioral change through a restructuring of identity and longer-term goals, and the short-term plans and daily activities in which one engages in pursuit of them.[34] McLean and Pratt note that turning points "are usually events in which one understands something new about oneself or faces decisions about different paths to take in life, [thus] the emphasis on self-reflection [is] particularly well suited to examine in relation to identity development."[35]

The mediation results further extend previous research in that they suggest a directionality of effects from reflecting on and discussing one's purpose in life to positive changes in goal direct-edness, which in turn predict benefits for life satisfaction. Much of the previous literature only suggests correlational relations among purpose and life satisfaction. However, directionality should be inferred from these data with caution, because the difference scores for goal directedness and life satisfaction are measurements taken at the same time point and thus do not represent temporal effects.

In addition, the findings of a direct effect of the purpose inter-view on life satisfaction, above and beyond that which may have occurred through goal directedness, suggest a process heretofore unexplored. Perhaps engaging in deep reflection on one's life goals provides an opportunity to integrate and assimilate one's goals, val-ues, plans, and behaviors in ways that go beyond mere goal direct-edness; such integration and assimilation may permit greater alignment between one's goals and one's identity (such as greater self-concordance), which is likely to predict later well-being.[36] These processes may further increase the likelihood of short-term goal attainment, which can lead to increased happiness.[37] Future research in this area would surely benefit from integrating assess-ments of self-concordance, goal attainment, and identity development.

Limitations and future directions
The findings of this study should be considered in the context of certain limitations. The generalizability of the results may be lim-ited, since all participants were in college. The college years are thought to afford a psychosocial moratorium during which greater identity exploration can take place; if the benefits of the purpose interview flow from the opportunity to engage more deeply in self-reflection, non-college-going emerging adults (who are more likely to be employed and have families) may not have the same luxury.[38] In addition, this study focused on only two components of purpose: purpose identification and goal directedness. According to Damon, Menon, and Bronk's definition, the self-transcendent nature of one's life goals was not assessed. It is possible that the

results may have been moderated by the content of one's life goals, such that they might be stronger for those who had primarily self-transcendent life goals relative to those who had primarily self-enhancing life goals.[39]

Implications

Although this work may perhaps be just a first step in the direction of purpose interventions, it nevertheless presents exciting possibilities for practical applications within and outside educational contexts. Indeed, one of the most appealing aspects of using the purpose discussion to enhance goal directedness and life satisfaction is that it does not require any special tools, significant investment in any products, or even much time. Practically anyone—a teacher, youth worker, or parent—can initiate it. The only conditions that are necessary to be in place are about forty-five minutes of the young person's and adult's time and the willingness of the young person to talk about what is most important to him or her.

In this study, the interviewers had no prior affiliation with the participants, suggesting that the initiator of the purpose discussion need not be particularly close to the young person. The initiator need not even be an adult. Provided that the discussion follows the general guidelines of interviewing used here and the initiator of the discussion is capable of eliciting genuine reflection, such a discussion could be shared between two young people; indeed, properly structured, such a discussion could be bidirectional, and thus likely to have benefits for each young person.

In educational settings, the purpose discussion might be integrated into student affairs practice in colleges, such as in career counseling or academic advising sessions, which in many colleges happen at least once a year and can last from thirty to sixty minutes. In the high school setting, a shortened version of the purpose discussion could easily be introduced in a conversation between a student and a guidance counselor, or perhaps a teacher integrating opportunities for such reflection into class projects or assignments. Although it is likely that engaging in the purpose discussion just once will have benefits that last many months, it may be advisable to arrange semiregular discussions of purpose so that the reflection process is ongoing.

Beyond the school setting, and likely of even greater potential impact, regular purpose-oriented conversations in the home, especially among young people and their parents, may engender significant benefits in terms of young people's goal directedness and satisfaction with their lives. Youth workers across domains, from community leaders to coaches, could regularly ask young people to reflect on their involvements and how they might be serving their longer-term goals. Ideally, the purposeful strivings of young people would be shared among all adults in a young person's life across domains, increasing the likelihood of targeted and sustained support for the young person's purposeful pursuits. While a one-time purpose discussion can have important long-term benefits, it may be that forming ecologies supportive of purpose discussion and reflection is even more likely to set young people on the path to their purpose.

Notes

1. For example, Baumeister, R. F. (1991). *Meanings of life*. New York: Guilford Press; Damon, W., Menon, J., & Bronk, K. C. (2003). The development of purpose during adolescence. *Applied Developmental Science, 7*, 119–128; Ryff, C. D. (1989). Happiness is everything, or is it? Explorations on the meaning of psychological well-being. *Journal of Personality and Social Psychology, 57*, 1069–1081.

2. Astin, A. W. (2004). Why spirituality deserves a central place in liberal education. *Liberal Education, 90*, 34–41; Damon, W. (2008). *The path to purpose: Helping our children find their calling in life*. New York, NY: Simon & Schuster.

3. For example, Yeager, D. S., & Bundick, M. J. (2009). The role of purposeful work goals in promoting meaning in life and in schoolwork during adolescence. *Journal of Adolescent Research, 24*, 423–452.

4. Arnett, J. J. (2004). *Emerging adulthood*. New York, NY: Oxford University Press.

5. Damon. (2008); Luyckx, K., Goossens, L., & Soenens, B. (2006). A developmental contextual perspective on identity construction in emerging adulthood: Change dynamics in commitment formation and commitment evaluation. *Developmental Psychology, 42*, 363–380.

6. Settersten, R. A., Furstenberg, F. F., & Rumbaut, R. G. (2000). *On the frontier of adulthood: Theory, research, and public policy*. Chicago, IL: University of Chicago Press.

7. Frankl, V. E. (1963). *Man's search for meaning: An introduction to logotherapy.* New York, NY: Washington Square Press.

8. For example, Battista, J., & Almond, R. (1973). The development of meaning in life. *Psychiatry, 36,* 409–427; Baumeister. (1991).

9. Damon et al. (2003). P. 121.

10. Damon et al. (2003). P. 121.

11. Kashdan, T. B., & McKnight, P. E. (2009). Origins of purpose in life: Refining our understanding of a life well lived. *Psychological Topics, 18,* 303–316.

12. Damon et al. (2003).

13. Compton, W, C,, Smith, M. L., Cornish, K. A., & Qualls, D. L. (1996). Factor structure of mental health measures. *Journal of Personality and Social Psychology, 71,* 406–413; Zika, S., & Chamberlain, K. (1992). On the relation of meaning in life and psychological well-being. *British Journal of Psychology, 83,* 133–145.

14. Ryff, C. D. (1989); Steger, M. F., Frazier, P., Oishi, S., & Kaler, M. (2006). The Meaning in Life Questionnaire: Assessing the presence of and search for meaning in life. *Journal of Counseling Psychology, 53,* 80–93.

15. Sin, N. L., & Lyubomirsky, S. (2008). Enhancing well-being and alleviating symptoms with positive psychology interventions: A practice-friendly meta-analysis. *Journal of Clinical of Psychology, 65,* 467–487.

16. Emmons, R. A., & McCullough, M. E. (2003). Counting blessings versus burdens: An experimental investigation of gratitude and subjective well-being in daily life. *Journal of Personality and Social Psychology, 84,* 377–389; Fordyce, M. W. (1983). A program to increase happiness: Further studies. *Journal of Counseling Psychology, 30,* 483–498; King, L. A. (2001). The health benefits of writing about life goals. *Personality and Social Psychology Bulletin, 27,* 798–807.

17. Steger, M. F. (2009). Meaning in life. In S. J. Lopez (Ed.), *Oxford handbook of positive psychology* (2nd ed., pp. 679–687). Oxford, UK: Oxford University Press.

18. Harrist, S., Carlozzi, B. L., McGovern, A. R., & Harrist, A. W. (2006). Benefits of expressive writing and expressive talking about life goals. *Journal of Research in Personality, 41,* 923–930.

19. MacLeod, A. K., Coates, E., & Hetherton, J. (2008). Increasing well-being through teaching goal-setting and planning skills: Results of a brief intervention. *Journal of Happiness Studies, 9,* 185–196.

20. See Damon. (2008).

21. See Damon. (2008).

22. Yeager, D. S., & Walton, G. M. (2011). Social-psychological interventions in education: They're not magic. *Review of Educational Research, 81*(2), 267–301.

23. Steger et al. (2006).

24. Steger et al. (2006).

25. Ryff. (1989).

26. Ryff. (1989). P. 1071.

27. Diener, E., Emmons, R. A., Larsen, R. J., & Griffin, S. (1985). The Satisfaction with Life Scale. *Journal of Personality Assessment, 49*, 71–75.
28. See Pavot, W., & Diener, E. (1993). Review of the Satisfaction with Life Scale. *Psychological Assessment, 5*, 164–172.
29. See Baron, R. M., & Kenny, D. A. (1986). The moderator-mediator variable distinction in social psychological research: Conceptual, strategic, and statistical considerations. *Journal of Personality and Social Psychology, 51*, 1173–1182.
30. Preacher, K. J., & Hayes, A. F. (2004). SPSS and SAS procedures for estimating indirect effects in simple mediation models. *Behavior Research Methods, Instruments, and Computers, 36*, 717–731.
31. Arnett. (2004).
32. Graber, J. A., & Brooks-Gunn, J. (1996). Navigating the passage from childhood through adolescence. *Developmental Psychology, 32*, 768–776. P. 772.
33. McLean, K. C., & Pratt, M. W. (2006). Life's little (and big) lessons: Identity statuses and meaning-making in the turning point narratives of emerging adults. *Developmental Psychology, 42*, 714–722.
34. Elder, G. (1998). The life course as developmental theory. *Child Development, 69*, 1–12; McAdams, D. P. (1993). *The stories we live by: Personal myths and the making of the self.* New York, NY: Morrow.
35. McLean & Pratt. (2006). P. 715.
36. Sheldon, K. M., & Elliot, A. J. (1999). Goal striving, need-satisfaction, and longitudinal well-being: The Self-Concordance Model. *Journal of Personality and Social Psychology, 76*, 482–497.
37. Sheldon, K. M., & Houser-Marko, L. (2001). Self-concordance, goal-attainment, and the pursuit of happiness: Can there be an upward spiral? *Journal of Personality and Social Psychology, 80*, 152–165.
38. Schwartz, S. J., Côté, J. E., & Arnett, J. J. (2005). Identity and agency in emerging adulthood: Two developmental routes in the individualization process. *Youth and Society, 37*, 201–229; Settersten et al. (2000).
39. Yeager & Bundick. (2009).

MATTHEW J. BUNDICK *is director of research at the Quaglia Institute for Student Aspirations and adjunct assistant professor at the University of Pittsburgh.*

The author discusses practical ways that educators, researchers, and policymakers can support youth purpose.

7

Conclusion: Recommendations for how practitioners, researchers, and policymakers can promote youth purpose

Jenni Menon Mariano

THIS VOLUME OF *New Directions for Youth Development* offers compelling recommendations for practitioners, researchers, and policymakers. One of the most heartening findings is that there are plenty of strategies that teachers can easily incorporate into what they are already doing in the classroom. These approaches do not require specific training or expertise. For example, in the first article, Sonia Issac Koshy and Jenni Menon Mariano describe how academic subject matter was used in a college classroom to discuss purpose, showing how teachers can devise creative ways to integrate teaching for purpose into their current curriculum. Also, several instruments have already been developed to study purpose, and these can double as classroom tools. For example, teachers can engage their students in reflective exercises and class discussions about their purposes in life using youth purpose interviews described by Matthew J. Bundick in the sixth article and discussion strategies that Jane Elizabeth Pizzolato, Elizabeth Levine Brown, and Mary Allison Kanny describe in the fifth article. This can be done at any school level, ranging from elementary school to college. Purpose interviews, reflections, and discussions can be used by guidance and career counselors. Similarly, schools can use the purpose survey methodologies described in the third article, by Devora Shamah, and the fifth article to assess their students' purpose levels and address them accordingly.

Short activities, such as the value card sort that Bryan J. Dik, Michael F. Steger, Amanda Gibson, and William Peisner describe in the fourth article, are easily used with children of all ages. Their activity has students sort and reflect on work values that can translate into positive career purposes. Educators can also modify the card content to encourage other types of purposes. Students, for example, might sort values pertaining to school and community life or social change at higher levels, and then imagine ways that they can contribute to making these values a reality. Values pertaining to youths' participation in sports, the arts, and other in-school- and out-of-school-time activities might also be employed. Another short activity that Pizzolato, Brown, and Kanny propose is to have students develop a timeline for achieving small goals that lead up to their purposes and then identify people in their lives who can support them.

These strategies can go far in supporting young people's purpose development. Armed with these tools, teachers should be encouraged to include their students' purpose development in classroom action research projects. To take this one step further, educators can engage whole classrooms and schools, including staff, in these purpose activities, with the aim of creating a sense of community purpose. Purpose discussions among school community members are useful. School community members might create Pizzolato, Brown, and Kanny's purpose timeline for the whole institution, so that the individual classroom, or the whole school, is the unit of analysis. Games like the One Village Game described by Dik, Steger, Gibson, and Peisner could contribute to a unity and ethic of purpose when played in a whole-school or cross-class-room context.

When students actively participate in the development of community purpose in these ways, collective plans of action around these purposes are more likely to evolve organically from students' concerns and interests. Students are less likely to feel that community actions are imposed from outside without involving them. Pizzolato, Brown, and Kanny, for instance, discuss how important it is for youth to be able to connect positive images of themselves, in the future and the present, with current school behavior. As Kendall Cotton Bronk demonstrates in the second article, developing an identity and developing purpose may occur together, so that attempts to inspire young people's dedication to prosocial purposes need to take each young person's unique sense of self into mind. Fortunately, Koshy and Mariano profile a school program that structures its curriculum specifically around having students design service activities around shared community purposes of their choosing—showing that constructing such a program is indeed viable. Thus, student participation in community purpose development is a promising way for educators to help students connect their personally meaningful goals with contributions to a proximal environment that is greater than themselves (the school community) and one that they experience on an everyday basis. Perhaps, as Shamah's findings in article 3 suggest, school policies that allow youth to earn credit for apprenticeships and service-learning activities would provide more purpose development opportunities.

Practitioners need not stop at the school level. Many strategies can be replicated at the community level too. For example, parents can use purpose discussions with their children, out-of-school-time and religious organizations can use them in their youth programming, and youth-led organizations can encourage these discussions among peers.

Educators should be aware too that the implicit curriculum is just as powerful in promoting, or neglecting, purpose instruction. As Shamah highlights, sports teams provide forums where many youth learn about purpose by the way that coaches promote coop-eration among team members rather than the personal glory of any of its single members. As Shamah notes, however, to serve the diversity of young people's interests, communities should provide a wealth of opportunities for young people to explore and practice purpose. Those opportunities can come in the form of work, school, or extracurricular activities. Still, providing the venue is not enough. Such experiences need to place youth in positions of responsibility and decision making. Also, in all of these experi-ences, communities need to think about how to promote intergen-erational respect and collaboration.

Implications for research

From a research perspective, the articles in this volume set a foun-dation for future progress. To date, the youth purpose interview method has been developed and is being used in research. Researchers should certainly continue to use this type of measure, but they also need shorter measures that can cut down on time and cost. As some of the article authors note, several valid and reliable survey methods for youth are now available too and might be used in this way. However, it is critical to recognize that many of these measures capture only part of what purpose is—usually by focus-ing on one aspect of the construct, such as personal meaning or goal directedness, and they fail to capture purpose in its full glory. It is questionable, for instance, whether youth purpose exemplars, who do exhibit purpose in its full glory, would score differently on current measures than peers with more moderate purpose manifes-tations. While this remains an empirical question that has not been studied, it will be best answered with a valid purpose measure.

Also, the more established purpose survey measures tend to focus on a general sense of purpose and do not identify the specific content of young people's purposes. Knowing purpose content, however, is important in helping practitioners identify young peo-ple's interests, and research to date suggests that purpose may be best supported when that support connects with the individual's own interests. Furthermore, knowing the content is important in assessing the positive or negative directions of one's purpose. While this volume has focused on noble purpose, purpose by definition can also be antisocial in nature while still seeking to contribute to the world beyond self. A host of destructive causes in human history serve as examples . Of course, any self-report measure that seeks to gauge the pro- or antisocial status of individuals' purposes is bound to be at risk for socially desirable responding. Therefore, researchers need to devise ways to get around this issue, perhaps by designing accompanying informant measures or observational measures that researchers and practitioners can use reliably across settings.

Research on youth purpose would benefit from even greater collaboration between researchers and educators. School remains a serious field of endeavor in instructing for purpose, so research will fare well if more teachers and schools open their classrooms and institutions to the long-term study of youth purpose. This connects to a central focus that researchers need to take. Researchers should increasingly focus their efforts on studying not just the condition of purpose within the individual, but on the settings in which young people are embedded and how those settings can support purpose development. Ecological, developmental, and dynamic systems perspectives are helpful in informing these types of investigations and represent cutting-edge theoretical frameworks that researchers can use.

Researchers must now expand the study of youth purpose support to wider populations of young people. This volume is a start in that direction through a foray into purpose with rural populations, youth of varying ages, and youth from diverse ethnic and social backgrounds. Yet much more needs to be done. One central question is whether different cultures of purpose exist, each representing potentially viable pathways to positive development, and whether those cultures thus require different supports. Emerging research suggests that youth with arts purposes may fall into this set. Measuring the beyond-the-self aspect of purpose in this group is problematic when using an a priori definition of the concept.[1] When speaking of the impact of culture on purpose, it is clear that researchers will need to expand their study beyond American youth, including developing and testing measures internationally.

Implications for policy

Educational policymakers are in a strong position to help practitioners and researchers realize their goals for supporting youth purpose. In collaboration with researchers, they could rewrite the current student testing requirement to include purpose measurement and not just academic outcomes. This should not occur as a gauge of each school's ultimate efficacy or as a test of teacher performance, but as formative information for leaders at the school, district, state, and national levels. The information gathered could inform additional resource allocation for purpose instruction and encouragement. As the research in this volume suggests, however, purpose may be best fostered through providing opportunities for young people to think about, discuss, and then devise actions to engage their interests in authentic ways within a social context. Social policymakers can contribute accordingly by making sure all schools and communities have access to the people and organizations through which purposes can emerge. Because youth spend large portions of their waking moments in school, educational funding policies should address schools' ability to maintain a breadth of activities and courses to address positive purpose development. Schools should be furnished with adequate numbers of counselors and mentors who can initiate purpose conversations with students.

Where schools do not address the needs, social policies should consider how to support community programs that do. Communities need places where youth can engage their interests toward the social good, such as youth organizations that promote potential purpose content like civic engagement, the arts, and faith-based programs. Young people who do not have them should be given access to resources that will enable them to take advantage of these opportunities; such resources may include transportation or the material resources to take part in the community programs.

Similarly, teacher accreditation agencies and departments of education can encourage teacher-training programs to incorporate skill building in purpose promotion. Instead of viewing this challenge as just one more thing to add to the teacher-training curriculum, this volume has shown how instructing for purpose is easily integrated into what educators are already doing, and the same can apply to teacher education programs. For example, psychological foundations courses in teacher education already deal with developmental tasks at each age across childhood, and purpose is one of these in key theories. In many cases, colleges and universities may be surprised to find that integrating purpose into the teacher education curriculum falls naturally in line with their mission, values, and goals.

Note
1. Malin, H. (2011, June 23.) Personal communication.

JENNI MENON MARIANO *is an assistant professor of educational psychology and human development at the University of South Florida Sarasota-Manatee.*

Index

NEW DIRECTIONS FOR YOUTH DEVELOPMENT

ORDER FORM SUBSCRIPTION AND SINGLE ISSUES

DISCOUNTED BACK ISSUES:

Use this form to receive 20% off all back issues of *New Directions for Youth Development*.
All single issues priced at **$23.20** (normally $29.00)

TITLE	ISSUE NO.	ISBN

Call 888-378-2537 or see mailing instructions below. When calling, mention the promotional code JBNND to receive your discount. For a complete list of issues, please visit www.josseybass.com/go/ndyd

SUBSCRIPTIONS: (1 YEAR, 4 ISSUES)

☐ New Order   ☐ Renewal

U.S.	☐ Individual: $89	☐ Institutional: $281
CANADA/MEXICO	☐ Individual: $89	☐ Institutional: $321
ALL OTHERS	☐ Individual: $113	☐ Institutional: $355

Call 888-378-2537 or see mailing and pricing instructions below.
Online subscriptions are available at www.onlinelibrary.wiley.com

ORDER TOTALS:

Issue / Subscription Amount: $ _____

Shipping Amount: $ _____
(for single issues only – subscription prices include shipping)

Total Amount: $ _____

SHIPPING CHARGES:	
First Item	$6.00
Each Add'l Item	$2.00

(No sales tax for U.S. subscriptions. Canadian residents, add GST for subscription orders. Individual rate subscriptions must be paid by personal check or credit card. Individual rate subscriptions may not be resold as library copies.)

BILLING & SHIPPING INFORMATION:

☐ **PAYMENT ENCLOSED:** *(U.S. check or money order only. All payments must be in U.S. dollars.)*

☐ **CREDIT CARD:**   ☐ VISA   ☐ MC   ☐ AMEX

Card number _____Exp. Date_____

Card Holder Name_____Card Issue # _____

Signature _____Day Phone_____

☐ **BILL ME:** *(U.S. institutional orders only. Purchase order required.)*

Purchase order # _____
Federal Tax ID 13559302 • GST 89102-8052

Name_____

Address_____

Phone_____ E-mail_____

Copy or detach page and send to: **John Wiley & Sons, One Montgomery Street, Suite 1200,
San Francisco, CA 94104-4594**

Order Form can also be faxed to: **888-481-2665**

PROMO JBNND

Notes for Contributors

After reading this issue, you might be interested in becoming a contributor to *New Directions for Youth Development: Theory, Practice, and Research*. In the tradition of the New Directions series, each volume of the journal addresses a single, timely topic, although special issues covering a variety of topics are occasionally commissioned. Submissions should address the implications of theory for practice and research directions, and how these arenas can better inform one another. Articles may focus on any aspect of youth development; all theoretical and methodological orientations are welcome.

If you would like to serve as an issue editor, you can email the editor-in-chief, Gil Noam, at Gil_Noam@harvard.edu. If he approves of your idea, the next step would be to submit an outline of no more than three pages that includes a brief description of your proposed topic and its significance, along with a brief synopsis of individual articles (including tentative authors and a working title for each chapter).

If you are interested in contributing an individual article, please contact the managing editor Erin Cooney at ecooney@mclean.harvard.edu first to see whether the topic will fit with any of the upcoming issues. The upcoming issues are listed on our Web site, www.pearweb.org/ndyd. If the article does fit topically, the managing editor will send you guidelines for submission.

For all prospective issue editors:

• Please make sure to keep accessibility in mind, by illustrating theoretical ideas with specific examples and explaining technical terms in nontechnical language. A busy practitioner who may not have an extensive research background should be well served by our work.

- Please keep in mind that references should be limited to twenty-five to thirty per article. Authors should make use of case examples to illustrate their ideas, rather than citing exhaustive research references. For readers who want to delve more deeply into a particular topic, you and/or chapter authors may want to recommend two or three key articles, books, or Web sites that are influential in the field, to be featured on a resource page.
- All reference information should be listed as endnotes, rather than including author names in the body of the article or footnotes at the bottom of the page. The endnotes are in APA style.
- Please visit http://www.pearweb.org for more information.

Gil G. Noam
Editor-in-Chief